You Will Never Be Funny

An Introduction to Improvised Comedy

Drew McCreadie

4th edition

You Will Never Be Funny

youwillneverbefunny@strangeinthehead.com

ISBN: 9798749565249

DEDICATION

To my fellow professional improvisors:
Without you I wouldn't have to share the limelight,
But then, there would be none.

Special thanks to Sue Whitehead
who did the proofreading
to make suer their wear no mitsakes.
(You mised some.)

Table of Contents

FORWARD

I first worked with Mr. McCreadie when I made it to *MainStage* at *Vancouver Theatresports League* in 2003.

I remember him being incredibly outspoken and incredibly funny. Through the years Drew and I have performed together many times in Vancouver in various improv troupes, including *Canadian Comedy Award* winners, *Urban Improv.*

(I actually just got back from Thailand where Drew and I did some improv in Bangkok to a sold out house.)

Being onstage with Drew is never boring. His style is both arresting and offensive, yet somehow charming and truthful, which I am sure you will discover from reading this book.

In 2014, I became the Artistic Director of *Vancouver Theatresports League*, the largest professional improvised comedy theatre company in Vancouver. The company is known for packed houses and very experienced and hilarious performers.

I got into improv because it terrified me. It still does. Nearly every time I go onstage I still get crazy stomach flips. That's what I love about improv. It never gets tired and delivers unmitigated fun every time I do it.

For beginners improv can be difficult because life is usually led, quite successfully, by planning ahead. The death of improv is planning....so throwing yourself into something with no plan is ‘f’ing scary. But the reward of it is ‘f’ing awesome.

Improv isn't just for people who want to entertain. Improv is great for life, in general. Trust me on that one.

So go do it. Don't wait. Oh... and let Drew show you how.

His book offers a very practical approach for beginners, while discussing some of the theory behind improv and comedy in general.

He's one of the most frank and funny teachers I know. I am sure you will find this book very valuable, and hope you enjoy it as much as I will...when I read it.

Kidding!

Am I?

Seriously, this book is great. Now go do improv and save the world.

Denise Jones
Artistic Director
Vancouver Theatresports League

Introduction to The Fourth Edition

Four editions later and there are still typos. It blows my mind! Anyway... enough about that.

The title of this work is the true key to unlocking the door to the proper headspace you need to be in to learn to do improv well. Unfortunately, I can not explain to you exactly what I mean. You need to figure out what I mean for yourself. And you can only do that by experiencing improv.

But I can give you a hint: I am talking about you, not other people who might also be reading this book.

With this book I hope to trick you into having a deeper understanding of what is unlearnable about improv.

People desperately want to be funny. Being funny is a virtue, for sure. And there are some who try improv as a way of becoming the funny person they wish they were. I am often surprised that those who throw themselves so completely into chasing this dream are often those who are least likely to ever achieve the goal. Perhaps it should not be surprising at all, as these naturally unfunny sorts must, on some subconscious level, see the deficiency in themselves (their lack of humour), and want to correct that flaw. Which is fine. Which is great actually... as long as you recognize and admit to yourself that that is what is going on.

An unfunny person that knows it can learn something. The problem is when you think you are funny and are not, and head into improv (or any other type of comedy) with this delusion boldly held as fact, for it will be this exact delusion that will prevent you from learning what you need to learn, experiencing what you need to experience, and growing where you need to grow. You will never be funny! Accept that, then you can learn to be.

If you are already funny, then you can ignore all that... as long as you are not deluding yourself.

Cheers, and good luck.

Drew

Ps. If you find any typos email them to me.

SOME QUESTIONS BEFORE WE BEGIN

What Is Improv?

Improvisation is the art of making stuff up on the spot. This book focuses *on improvised comedy* or *improv*, and by that I mean a group of performers (improvisors) who step onto stage with no script and do something funny. They may very well have an idea of what they will do in a general sense, but what they will actually say, what they will actually do, and what the final story will be, is completely unknown, and will not be known until it is all over. To many people, even professional actors, this idea can be terrifying. Even madness. Glorious madness! And when it works, it is exhilarating.

This book is designed to show you how to make it work. You're welcome.

Different Forms, But One Root

There are many forms of improv within the improv comedy world. There is *long form, short form, games or handles, competitive improv, improvised plays and musicals*, and *parody improv*, to name a few. (There is even improv that is not comedy – and I mean on purpose! This is often used as part of a therapy program for troubled youth, or by the American government on prisoners at secret torture bases throughout the world.) Each has a different form and structure, but the root of all the different forms is the same: *making stuff up on the spot*. As a beginner improvisor, the skills you develop will be equally useful in any of the various forms that are out there. Learn and develop good habits as early on as possible, so that regardless of what kind of improv show you end up performing in, you will feel comfortable, and the improvisation will come to you more and more effortlessly.

If you are not interested in actually ever performing improv, remember this: you might become interested. Even if you don't ever set foot on stage, the skills you can learn from doing improv can translate into real advantages in other fields. Someone who is quick-witted, able to adapt instantly, and can handle whatever is thrown in their path effortlessly and with lightning speed is someone who could be a benefit to any profession (the duct-tape thinkers at NASA's Apollo 13 mission, for example, pop to mind). Learn to do improv, and become more of that kind of person.

Barprov

My main focus will be imparting some of the knowledge and wisdom I have gained over my years as a professional improvisor, concentrating almost primarily on *improvised sketch comedy* (as opposed to improvised drama or tragedy, or astrophysics), and in particular, a type of improvisation that we in the Vancouver improv community sometimes refer to as *Barprov*. Much of my time as a professional improvisor has been spent performing in a bar or cabaret setting. This poses its own challenges, such as competition with the noise of drinks being made, drunks being drunks, and the table at the back talking amongst themselves very loudly about the humdrum boredom that is their pathetic lives outside of theatre.

The features of *Barprov,* then, are those techniques that allow you to grab the attention of the audience quickly, get to the funny, and get the hell out before anyone knows what hit them. If you can master *Barprov*, I contend, you will soar when offered the opportunity to perform in a more theatrical setting, with an audience that is more attentive, less distracted, soberer, and with at least a basic understanding of the decorum of a theatre. I am not sure that audience actually exists, but we can always dream!

Who Can Use This Book?

This book can be used by anyone, especially someone with a table that has one leg shorter than another: just stuff this book right underneath. (Unless you bought the e-book version, in which case I suggest you buy yourself an e-table.)

This book is designed for beginners who are interested in learning the art of performing live improvised comedy and experiencing the glorious thrill of having a roomful of people laugh at what you say... and in a good way. For those with some improv experience, this book may serve as a reminder of things forgotten, or perhaps be a means by which you can come to understand what you already know. Whatever the case, I think you should definitely buy it.

Improv Is Useful Everywhere

Additionally, improvisation is a very useful skill in a variety of non-performance related fields, like real jobs and stuff like that. Your average businessperson can gain a lot from adapting the fundamental principles of improvisation to the humdrum boredom that is a life in business (I can only assume, as I avoid it like the plague, which, I equally avoid like a life with a real job.) I have included, as an appendix, an article on improv in the workplace that I wrote for a project management website. That's for you business types.

Can Everyone Learn To Be Funny?

No.

Can Everyone Learn To Do Improv Comedy?

Maybe. Being funny is a good start. But it is not completely necessary, and it is also not a guarantee of success in improv; being naturally funny is simply not enough. There are some fundamental principles and techniques to improv that help to solve the inevitable problems that arise when two or more people try to create something together. Further, these principles not only help performers to overcome obstacles, they actually help in the creation process by providing a loose framework upon which great ideas can be built. (It is this aspect of improv comedy that is most useful to those outside of the performance world.)

You Can Learn to Do Things That Are Funny

I believe, with concentration and effort, most people can learn improvisation to some degree. Improvisational comedy, when done properly, is funny. It has funny built in, as I will discuss shortly. At the very least, improv done correctly can be entertaining. It is fun to watch people being good at something; it is enjoyable to watch a group of people achieving something together. This is why people like sports, I guess. Sport, as my friend Roland once said in an attempt to make me understand why anyone would squander their time with it, is the ultimate improv because you don't know how the game will end until the game is over.... I guess. Whatever, Roland.

You Will Never Be Funny

But if you are not funny, you never will be. Get used to it. Get over it. And for the love of all that is mythical, stop trying to be funny: You are just making things worse!

So this book will not teach you how to be funny. It will teach you how to do things that are often funny to watch. It will teach you how to do things that are fun to do. It will make you smarter, maybe. It may also destroy some of your intellect. Ah well. Easy come, easy go.

Nothing will ever make you funnier. If you are not funny now, you will never be funny. If you are someone who is not funny but wants to be, ask yourself why you want to be funny. You can not learn to be funny.

Why Do You Think You Are Funny?

If you think you are funny, ask yourself why you think that. I have met many people who think they are funny and I often wonder what or who gave them that idea. Does your mother say you are funny? 'Cause that doesn't count! Are people laughing after you say something? Are they? Really? Do they laugh more as you walk away? That's a different thing, you know? Remember: a joke needs to have other people find it funny; if only you find it funny, then *you* are the joke.

Ok.... One Way To Become Funnier

Ok. There is *one* thing that can make you funnier. *Self-confidence*: Real self-confidence -- not overcompensating self-confidence which has the very opposite effect. Insecurity is the opposite of funny. Perhaps that bears repeating: insecurity is the *opposite* of funny! And insecurity shines like a super-nova when you try to overcompensate for your insecurities by pretending to be self-confident. It's awful!

If you can make a conscious decision to *no longer fear looking like the idiot you already are*, then maybe you can be a little bit funnier. Maybe.

Real funny takes guts.

THE THEORETICAL STUFF:
THE NATURE OF COMEDY

What is Comedy?

Let's get right to it. What is comedy? You can *Google* a definition if you want. I was going to do it and then add it here, but my Internet is down... so I will leave it up to you. You might have heard that *comedy is all about timing* (said with a long pause before the word timing.) Yeah. I guess. But I have my own definition. ***Comedy is a pleasant surprise.*** Nice and short. Now here comes an outrageously long explanation of what I mean...

Surprise

The essential part of comedy is *the unexpected.* If you see it coming, often it is not that funny. That's why a joke is less funny the second time you hear it. (I will discuss what seems like an exception to this later on, so wait for it.)

Improv Has Surprise Built-in

For me, *surprise*, the absolutely necessary part of comedy, is the hardest part, and the most fun. *Surprise* is something that improv comedy does well; because improv involves several performers working together on a stage to create a scene, and because you have no idea what the other person will say, there is a built-in level of *surprise* to any improv scene. Not only is the audience surprised, but the performers often are as well. Professional improvisors work on deliberately expanding their imaginations, and attempt to take scenes on unexpected tangents for this very reason. They use exercises that attempt to train their brains to think in different ways, hoping to unleash new imaginative connections and insights that will surprise and delight the audience and their fellow performers.

Surprising Yourself

This necessary element of *surprise* is what makes comedy writing so difficult. If you have never done it, consider this: You are sitting in front of a blank computer screen, or with a blank sheet of paper, and you are trying to write something surprising. You are literally trying to *surprise yourself!* That is why you will hear writers talk about *writers' block*, which, to non-writers, may sound like the whinge of a lazy artiste... which it is, but it is also something quite real, and incredibly frustrating. Surprising yourself is not easy. This may be why so many writers drink or do drugs, in an attempt to alter their consciousness so that they will have a new, different, and surprising thought.

Exercise 1.0

Take a moment and try to write a joke... even a simple one.

Knock, Knock. Who's there? ________________.

Or,

Why did the chicken cross the road?

To ________________.

Try to write something that surprises you, something that you would never ever think of! Not *the first thing that pops into your mind,* because obviously you would think of that, you just did.

Now, have money for food and rent only if you are able to do it.

Welcome to the life of a comedy writer!

Surprise Is The Result of Accessing Your Imagination

Surprise is inextricably connected to imagination, and the freer and quicker we are able to access our imagination, the more surprising we can be. The best improvisors have direct, unfettered access to their own imaginations. The worst improvisors travel down the same well-worn paths that others before them have traveled, confusing the successes of others as the route to their own success, not realizing that it was the act of hacking the path out of the jungle of the never-before-considered, and not the direction this path took, that was funny.

This book will discuss *surprise* in more detail throughout, as it is, in my view, the single most important element of comedy. I will give you some exercises and techniques that will help to build your surprise muscle (sounds somewhat dirty, deliberately), and offer some suggestions to overcome things that we all do naturally that work against directly accessing our imaginations. It's like finding your inner-child, but I hate kids, so I want nothing to do with them, inner or outer! I call it *Connecting with Your Imagination and Overcoming The Blocks That the Assholes of The World Have Been Throwing Up In Front Of You Your Whole Life.*

Pleasantries

Comedy is a pleasant surprise. The *pleasant* part of my definition is a little less obvious perhaps than the *surprise* part. *Pleasant* can mean different things to different people. We all know what an *un*pleasant surprise is: A higher than expected bill is a simple and universal example. Boooo. Not comedy.

Pleasant is Different for Everyone

For me, *pleasant* can mean many things. To each person *pleasant* is a little different, but there are a number of things that we all commonly find *pleasant*. Obviously, it is within this commonality that you are going to find the most mass appeal for your comedy. Here is my non-exhaustive list of things that I find *pleasant* in a comedic sense. Your list will likely include some from my list, and may include others as well.

Smart things
Witty things
Naughty things
Rebellious or freeing things
Sexy things
Juvenile, or childish things
Vindicating things

Recognize What is Pleasant for You

Finding and recognizing what is *pleasant* for you is vital to becoming a good improvisor. Understanding what makes your comedy tick will give you insight into your own comedic sensibilities, which in turn, will give you a better chance of developing your own unique style, a vital aspect of any successful performance career. It will also offer you some indications of where you might be weak and need more conscious focus. Being well rounded is a good thing in life (just ask your parents) but even more important in improv where a cursory knowledge on every topic imaginable can come in very, very handy.

Be Well Rounded

Be as well-rounded an improvisor as you can be. Be able to sing a little, dance a little, rap a little, do accents a little, do physical clowning a little, mime a little, and sword-fight a little. Know a little about math, science, movies, TV, politics, medicine, religion, philosophy, sports, geography, cosmology, astrology, dentistry, current events and shoe repair. Get on it.

Recognize What is Pleasant for Your Audience

Instantly recognizing what is *pleasant* for your audience is essential for becoming a good performer. Don't do dick jokes for the church group, funny as dicks and church groups are. That kind of thing.

Comedy is a pleasant surprise. Be surprising. Be pleasantly surprising.

Unpleasant Surprises

Being *pleasantly surprising* does not necessarily mean being pleasant. Comedy is often very dark, and for many of us the best comedy is found right there on the edge, the line between pleasant and unpleasant, between the *should* and *shouldn't*. Knowing where that line is can be super helpful!

People who often step over the line usually don't know where the line is. It is very <u>unpleasant</u> (*cringeworthy*, I call it) watching a performer who doesn't know where the line lies for a given situation, and therefore, when they trip over it, it is *not* comedy. You can often get away with stepping over the line on purpose, but are rarely forgiven for stepping over the line by accident. Sounds unfair. Welcome to life.

If you know you are stepping over the line, people will be more apt to go along with you for the ride, giving you the benefit of the doubt that you are being politically incorrect or in some way disregarding of social norms or etiquette for a reason (to make a political or satirical point, for example). If you trip accidently over the line of decorum, you expose yourself, your preconceptions, your biases, and your prejudices to the common opinion of the crowd. If your position is not in-line with your audience's, you will have instantly alienated yourself from those you need to endear yourself to.

A Punch In The Face

A punch in your face is not a pleasant surprise, and therefore not comedy. A punch in someone else's face *might* be, for several reasons:

1) It's not your face. (Sounds like a joke, but never underestimate the pleasantness of negativity directed away from yourself); and
2) *Justice* – maybe what's-his-name deserved it.

There is a strange cathartic experience that happens when we see others injure themselves, fall over, or otherwise find themselves in a situation we would greatly like to avoid. It's the pie in the face, the slip on the banana peel. Of course there is a limit to it, as something that is truly tragic (someone sustaining a terrible injury) quickly jumps into the realm of the unfunny. This slap-stick, pie in the face, ball to the groin type of humour is very low level, and is probably a remnant of some Neanderthal instinct... but we all still have it. And a great part of what makes it funny is that it didn't happen to us, it happened to someone else.

Likewise, seeing justice done is *pleasant*. Surprise justice can often be very funny, instant karma as it is sometimes called. I recently watched a YouTube video of an obnoxious driver tailgating someone else, giving them the finger and then, because he was focusing on being an asshole, ended up spinning out of control and ending up in a ditch. It was *surprising*. Check. And it was vindicating of the idea that tailgating is jerk-behaviour and is likely to cause an accident. *Pleasant by way of vindication*. Check. Therefore: Funny. The fact that no one got killed, especially not an innocent bystander was important too, of course, as that would quickly push the surprise into the unpleasant realm.

Dark Comedy

Now there is bound to be someone who, upon reading the last sentence, will say, with a smug 'They won't expect me to say this' look on his face, "If someone innocent had died then it wouldn't have been funny, it would have been hilarious."

First off, I *would* expect you to say something like that, you hackneyed asshole. And second, what's that about? It seems like an example of pure nastiness, and yet it is a very familiar thing to hear in comedy.

And can't comedy be nasty? I am sure you can think of some examples. Is that somehow proof that comedy does not need to be *pleasant*? Has someone already proved my definition of comedy wrong? Let's discuss. (The answer is *no*.)

Why is Nasty Sometimes Funny?

Let's start by taking the example of a sweet little fat kid getting kicked in the face with a ball and falling over. And by sweet little fat kid, I mean sweet, adorable, kind, never did anything to deserve it, trusting, freckly, redheaded, fat, little kid, getting a ball to the face and falling down. Maybe not your idea of funny? Ok. The reasons why you don't think it is funny are pretty obvious and so I will ignore them completely. We all get it. Let's talk about why it *is* funny, why something that seems unfair, unjust, and downright nasty might be funny. Where is the *pleasant* surprise necessary for it to be comedy by Drew's definition? It is obviously not *justice* in this case. Unless you *are* that sweet little fat kid, then it did happen to someone else, so there is that. But there is more to it than simply happening to someone else. But what?

Simple. The *pleasant* part in this case, for those that find it funny, is the exhilaration that people get from breaking the rules. It's the *pleasant* that comes from being rebellious: thinking, saying or doing that which you are not supposed to do. It is the *pleasant* that comes from forgiving yourself for not feeling guilty or bad. It is freeing because in a sudden instant you realize that you *can* say that, or do that. You can laugh at the poor little kid. Sure, you still *shouldn't* but you *can*! You just *did* and the world didn't end. It is freedom!

Freedom!!!!

Freedom is pleasant, and it is this freedom from the rules, social norms, and ethical and moral expectations that is the source of potential comedy from the nasty, mean, or inappropriate. Standup comics often pepper their routines with swear words and off-colour and/or taboo topics for this same motherfucking reason; it is a combination of shock-value (*surprise*) and *pleasantness* from a sense of freedom or wild abandon. 'I can't believe he said that!' which often means 'I am impressed by his courage to say that.'

Perhaps you have heard a comic say, "I am just saying what everybody else is thinking." That's what he's talking about: the joy of being free to speak your mind. The more uptight and controlled the culture in which you are performing comedy, the more choices you have on how to break the rules.

Dark and Dangerous

That does not mean that rebellious humour is funny to everyone. Every time you step into this realm -- the world of the taboo, inappropriate, touchy, or emotionally charged topics -- you run the risk, greater than with other topics, of not only missing the mark with your comedy, but of actually offending your audience, losing the good will of the crowd (which is vital for a successful show) and, in the worst case, turning them against you. You've been warned. (It is now that those people I discussed earlier, the ones who think they are funny without having ever been given any indication that they are, who more often than not, pipe up, indignant that their terrible, obvious, inappropriate joke was not appreciated, giving some lame, defensive, deflecting excuse that places the blame for the failure of *their* joke on the 'uptight audience'. Guess what I think of that.) There are many comedians who make a living by being offensive, but the successful ones all have three things in common: they know that they are being offensive, they know why it is offensive, and they are funny.

Improv Is Edgy

When discussing improv comedy, I think it is very important to recognize the challenges of *unpleasant* issues such as sexism, racism, nationalism, homophobia, and 'taboo' topics such as religion, rape, incest, child abuse, and the 'too-soon' references to tragedies, terrible illnesses and the like, because doing improv is *performance in the moment*, and as such, it needs a great deal of freedom from self-censorship. It is likely, therefore, that some or all of these issues will pop into mind at some time. If one hopes to quickly and directly access one's imagination there can be no time to second-guess yourself; you need to be free to say what comes to mind. On the other hand, the instantaneousness of it all is without time to reconsider, without the opportunity to check with others or compare what you are saying on stage in the heat of the performance with your own set of values. Improv is, therefore, devoid of the sober second thought that makes the Senates of the world the bastions of good, timely government! More than other forms of comedy, improv is, by its very improvised nature, more likely to send you into an area or topic that is potentially unpleasant or offensive to someone, and without time to plan in advance the likelihood of saying or doing something off-colour is high.

Know where your line is before you perform, and your stumbles across it will be less frequent. Because, on stage, you can't think before you speak, so think now before you think about speaking on stage.

Do As I Say, Not As I Do

In short, in improv, you sometimes say stuff you shouldn't; it just pops out. Avoiding this takes training, understanding your own boundaries (boundaries that you are willing to defend if you must), and playing at the very top of your intellect. It is easier said than done. I will offer some advice on how to try to achieve this lofty and important goal within this tome. I suggest you do as I say, not as I do on this one.

So that's what comedy is.

A SUPERFLITUDE OF MOMENTNESS

Not Sorry To Go Off On A Tangent

Improv is a team creative process, and as such differs in many fundamental ways from other creative processes such as writing, sculpting, painting or standup comedy, which are primarily solitary activities. The beauty of a team creative process, especially one with a goal of creating comedy, is that the very nature of collaboration creates unexpected results. Until we perfect the mind-reading device that the American CIA is undoubtedly working on, it is impossible to know exactly what someone else is thinking, and therefore, there is always an element of the unexpected when interacting with another person.

And we can, if we try, sometimes even *surprise* ourselves individually without relying on others. By practicing *tangential association*, that is, finding the connection between things that are not obviously connected, an improvisor can start to think new thoughts they have never had before. A good improvisor can do this often. Imagine a stage filled with performers who are all in a constant state of individual and group astonishment. It is glorious mayhem!

We find these *tangential associations* by allowing our minds to do it for us, almost subconsciously. We do that, by being *in the moment*.

Being In The Moment

When learning how to improvise, one of the first things you need to do is discover what it means to be *In The Moment*. Discovering and understanding this concept in an experiential way is the first step to the amazing possibilities of improv. The second step is to try and access that immediacy at will and to actually be *in the moment* as often as you can while on stage. This is definitely one of those *easier said than done* things.

Now Is All There Is

Being *in the moment* means a couple of things. First it means being present in the scene, and by this we mean to be actively listening and aware of what is happening *right now*, not thinking about where you hope the scene will go. It means *not* thinking about something funny to say. It means not thinking at all, actually. It is about reacting to what is happening now. What did your fellow improvisor just say? What is your character's response to that? Being *in the moment* involves active listening, and paying close attention to your fellow improvisors on stage.

Resist the Urge to Worry About What Happens Next

As a beginner improvisor there is an understandable desire to think ahead. You are on stage, hoping to be funny (your first mistake), and therefore your mind races around trying to think of something funny to say or do. You start to think about *how this scene might end*, what you will say when the other improvisor finally stops talking. It is natural, but completely wrong and terrible and awful and evil, but I don't want to come across judgmental, so I will just say that there is perhaps another way. As you may have guessed by my choice of words, a mind *racing around* is not what you need. You need a mind that is, at the risk of sounding artsy-fartsy spiritual, very calm and still. You achieve that through being *in the moment*. By focusing on what has *just happened* and what you are doing *right now*, you limit the racing that your mind can do.

You understand? No, you don't. You can not really understand until you have experienced it. An intellectual understanding doesn't really cut it. You need to have had the experience to know when you are having it. That is where improv exercises come in. Improv exercises are a way of practicing getting yourself *in the moment*, so that it becomes easier and easier to do over time. What follows are a series of exercises that are designed to help get people into the moment. I will describe the exercises, and what they hope to achieve, but really, they need to be experienced for the true learning to happen. Such is the absurdity of writing a book about something that needs to be experienced to be understood.

Exercise 1: Experiencing In The Momentness

First, I know *momentness* is not a word. It is underlined in red here on my word processor. Moving on.

The first of a series of exercises useful to demonstrating *'in the moment'* is a simple one. The group stands in a circle and passes around a mimed item, let's say a ball. As each person gets 'handed' the mimed item, they identify it, and then say a descriptive adjective about it. "This is a ball. And it is blue." The next person then does the same thing. "This is a ball. And it is big." Sounds very simple, and it is. What is the point of such an easy exercise? Slow down big wheel, I am getting to it.

Of course all the 'good' ideas get used up early. Someone says 'red' and all you are left with is *all the other colours of the spectrum*. This exercise must be allowed to carry on past the easy stage, when people have to start digging a little deeper for descriptive words. It is only then that the experience that improvisors need to have starts to manifest itself.

Now remember, that this is a *mimed item*, so it can have any adjective you want. "This is a ball. And it has eyes." So you have a completely *limitless* number of things you can say about it. In workshops, I even make the point that people can say contradictory things to what others have already established, that is: it is fine to say something is *blue* after someone else has said it is *green*; you can say it is *big* after someone else has told us it is *small*; and, you can even repeat what someone else said, technically, because no instruction was given forbidding it. You can even make up words ("It is a ball. And it is souplofty"), after all, people who make up words are better than other people because they have a superflitude of momentness!

Second Guessing

And here comes the point: even with a *universe* of possibilities, some of us still struggle a little when the item is passed to us. We struggle to come up with something 'good'. Worrying about it being 'good' is not being *in the moment*; it is being in the future, the aftermath, when people will be judging you based on what you said. Thinking about how something will be received in *not* being in the moment.

Pre-Planning Is Not Being In The Moment

To avoid not saying something 'good', to avoid not coming up with something smart and witty and interesting on the spot, some people (and by *some* I mean *most*, and by *most* I mean *everyone*) start *pre-planning*. Before the mimed item gets to them they start to think about what they will say when it is handed to them. Obviously *pre-planning* is not being *in the moment* either.

And here is the super-important, and perhaps counterintuitive lesson: The results of this pre-planning are <u>*not better*</u> than the results of just saying whatever comes to mind *in the moment*, especially in this exercise where you are allowed to say *absolutely* anything. There are *no* wrong answers at all, and yet, we struggle. This may at first seem counter intuitive as 'real life' seems to offer us countless examples of the opposite being true. But I assure you that the pre-planned response is *not* better than the *in the moment* response in improv. With work and practice the *in the moment* responses that you are able to conjure in the split of a second will become more and more satisfying to you.

Not **Being In The Moment** ***Risks Missing The Moment***

In this particular exercise it might not matter that you are ignoring everyone else during their turn while you hurriedly scan your memory banks to pre-plan for a funny adjective. But, if you are on stage, doing a scene with another person it does matter, it matters a superflitude! You need to be listening to them *actively*, and you cannot do that if you are pre-planning, worrying about saying something 'good', or doing any of a million other things that might keep you from being *in the moment.* (If you are wondering what I mean by *actively listening*, it is the opposite of what you do when your *significant other* is telling you about what happened to them at work today.) *Active listening* is not waiting for someone to stop talking so you can say what you have already decided you are going to say. *Active listening* is having no idea what you are going to say until you have heard what the other person has said.

After doing the exercise for a while, I ask the group to discuss what they felt they experienced, and I specifically ask how many would admit to *pre-planning*, or *worrying* about saying something '*good*'. Everyone except the liars puts up their hands.

Exercise2: Limiting Pre-Planning

We then do the exercise again, but this time, in an attempt to limit the amount of pre-planning that is possible, we add the instruction that the adjective you say *must be directly inspired by, or related to the adjective that the person* *immediately before you said*, ignoring anything that was said before that. This might sound something like:

"This is a cat. And it is yellow."
"This is a cat. It is red."
"This is a cat. And it is blue."
"This is a cat and it is sad."
"This is a cat. And it is depressed."
"This is a cat. And it is suicidal."
"This is a cat. And it is dead."
"This is a cat. And it is rotten."
"This is a cat. And it is smelly."
"This is a cat. And it is buried."

After a round of this we discuss again. Most people start to feel the difference between this and the previous exercise. This difference is the move toward being closer to *in the moment.*

"After Exercise Chat" Can Be Revealing

Let's look at the above example. *Yellow* is followed by *red* and *blue*. For most of us that seems obvious how each was inspired by the other. I wonder, however, if blue, (the third one) was not also inspired by yellow. It is impossible to know. Moving on.

Next we have *sad*, which when asked to explain, the improvisor who said it responded that to *be blue* is to *be sad*. Makes sense. And so on. *Depressed* comes from *sad*, and *suicidal* comes from *depression*. The point here is that improvisor number 6 could not pre-plan *suicidal* while improvisor number one was saying *yellow*. She needed to wait for the improvisor number 5 to say something (*depressed*) first. Much more *in the moment*. And *suicidal* is as good as anything she could have preplanned.

But let's look at improvisor number 10's statement: *buried*. Notice how it seems perhaps at first glance to make sense as part of a series *dead, rotten, smelly, buried*. But I would suggest that this improvisor may have failed in the task of being *in the moment*. How does *buried* relate to *smelly*? To my mind *buried* relates more to *dead*. It is like he heard dead and ignored the next two improvisors because he had already thought up *buried*. You don't bury smelly things, you bury dead things. (To clarify my point, ask yourself this: if I were to say to you out of the blue, not having anything to do with what you are reading now, "Say a word that relates to smelly?" what are the chances you would say *buried*? Low I would argue.)

Now remember that you can say anything, even contradictory things, so for improvisor 10 to say that the cat was *farty*, *dirty* or *unwashed*, thereby implying the cat was alive would have been fine. To my mind *farty*, *unwashed*, or *dirty* are all directly related to *smelly*, whereas *buried* is related to *dead*. Was the improvisor's mind pre-planning when he heard *dead* three improvisors before his turn? Or was he inspired by the combination of the three consecutive *dead*, *rotten* and *smelly* adjectives, which is completely understandable, but not per the instructions of the exercise. Perhaps, in *this* improvisor's mind, *smelly* does directly relate to *bury* in some way that I can't see. Perhaps, but I doubt it. We will never know; only he might know. Maybe he doesn't know. Maybe he doesn't really exist and this is just an example. Hopefully we have all learned something.

But I have experienced even clearer cases where it is more obvious that the improvisor is not *in the moment*, like for *kitten*, a series once went something like this: *small, tiny, sub-atomic, invisible, cute*. I am willing to bet anything that *cute* does not relate to, nor was it inspired by *invisible*. This improvisor was thinking about a cat, using her imagination to picture a cute cat, which is great... but she was *not* listening to the person directly before her who handed her a mimed *invisible* cat. She was not *actively listening*, and was not *in the moment.*

Popping Into The Imagination

Remember that this is a very specific exercise, where you are being asked to say something related to the thing said immediately before you *only,* and by consequence, to actively disregard what was said before that. In a scene, of course, what happened previously is going to have an effect on what you will say next. In a scene, it would make all sorts of *in the moment* sense to bury something that has been previously referred to as dead, rotten and smelly, and in contrast, to disregard dead and rotten, focusing on smelly only, might not be true to the scene.

Hopefully through this exercise, beginner improvisors are able to feel the difference between an idea that was pre-planned, and one that is allowed to pop into consciousness *in the moment*. The *in the moment* idea is what we are shooting for.

And that, folks, is the point of the exercise!

LETTING GO OF CONTROL

Experiencing *being in the moment* through exercises for the purpose of understanding on a deeper level what improvisors experience when performing, is step one. Step two, is to work on developing skills and techniques to allow yourself to be in that place often, and finally *always*, when on stage.

Being a Team Player

The single best way to become more present more of the time is to let go of the desire to *control*. This is more difficult for some people than for others. *Control freaks* naturally have the most difficulty; they are the ones that not only need to work the hardest to overcome their natural propensity, they are also the ones that *need* to overcome their natural propensity the most. Being a control freak on stage as part of an improv scene is a 100%, absolute, unqualified, iron-clad, full-money-back guarantee that what you will end up achieving will be inferior to what you could have achieved. (This can never be proved, but that doesn't make it any less true.)

You must learn to let go of control. If you cannot do it, improv is not for you. Try stand-up comedy where you get to be the writer, director, producer, and star of your own little 4 minute show. Improv is a team sport!

You Can Never Control Others

Here's why letting go of control is vital: You cannot control what other people on stage think, do, or say, and so trying to do so will always result in failure. It is impossible, and completely against the principles of improv if you try. If you need to be in control to feel comfortable then you will always feel uncomfortable: You must learn to be comfortable *not* being in control.

The following series of activities introduces this concept and offers an opportunity to practice this notion. These exercises should also give you examples of the superior end results that come from everyone on the team giving up control and embracing the team-based nature of improv comedy, as well as the pitfalls of not embracing this obligatory aspect.

The Gift Of Restrictions

At first we employ a number of activities and exercises that utilize *restrictions*, forcing us to *do* or *not do* something in some way, with the hope that the pressure in one direction will force us to spurt out comedic genius in the other. (An example of a restriction is doing a scene where every sentence must start with the letter 'S'.) These restrictions should be looked at as *gifts*, not as *constraints*; they should not limit our creativity in any way, but rather quite the contrary: By forcing us into some *new* area we are destined to think of or do something *new*; by restricting what we can do in a scene we are forced to come up with a new way of doing what needs to be done. In many ways, it is easier to perform when given restrictions, as complete openness can often be a bit overwhelming; (something that may have revealed itself when performing the first exercise, describing the mimed object.) Restrictions are like being given a goal, which serves many people well as a motivator for inspiration. Let's consider some example exercises.

Exercise 3: Sentence At A Time

This exercise is done in pairs, or a group of three if need be. The improvisors are instructed to stand facing each other and instructed to tell a story together. They are given a suggestion for the title of the story: <u>First Day At The Armory</u>, <u>When Susan Fell Off The Porch</u>, <u>How Marjorie Lost Her Arm</u>, <u>The Birthday Bicycle</u>, <u>Fred and Herman Find a Turtle</u>, or <u>Dan's Pet Pig</u>, or whatever. All the pairs are given the same story title. The restriction in this exercise is that each improvisor must each add to the story only one sentence at a time, alternating back and forth. They are given about a minute or two to do this, and are given a 10 second warning before bringing the exercise to a close. Again, a super simple task, but with the restriction that each improvisor can *only* say one sentence then must pass the story over to the other improvisor.

When they are done, one of the pair tells the rest of the group basically what happened in the story. Almost without fail these stories will be highly absurd, with very unusual and often nonsensical plot twists. There is often a lot of grossness and inappropriateness, mixed in with a liberal helping of magic and physical impossibilities. But none of this matters.

What matters in this activity is what the improvisors were able to observe about themselves while doing the exercise, and what they experienced.

Laughs Are a Good Sign

First thing that they will notice is that there is a lot of laughing. This is a good indication that there is a bit of comedy going on somewhere. It is not a comedy gun, but definitely comedy smoke. If asked why there is so much laughing, the answer is inevitably the same: At one or several points, the story veered off in a completely unexpected way, in a way that caught the other improvisor off guard. Surprise! See page 23.

The Fantastic World of Multiple Minds

I ask the improvisors if, left to do it individually, either of them would have come up with a story that was anywhere near as crazy. (What I am really asking is, *if left to themselves individually, could they come up with a story that would create as much laughter as their combined effort produced*? And I am not really asking them either, I am telling them that *they could not.* But I am doing it in a tricky, teachery way.) The answer almost always is *no,* with the odd exception of the smart-ass who wants everyone to know what a particularly unique and off-center imagination he/she has. (Imagine what I think of that.)

Usually the improvisors realize that by letting go of control, in this case *half of the story a sentence at a time*, the resulting story becomes much more surprising than anything they could think of by themselves.

This exercise is a good one as the improvisors need to be *in the moment*, as what they are going to say will be directly influenced by what the other improvisor has just said. It also teaches the thrill of letting go of control, and the resulting glorious mayhem that can be the result.

Then we take it up a notch.

Exercise 4: Word At A Time

To gain deeper understanding of the power of *letting go of control*, improvisors are asked to take it to the next level by telling a story, alternately speaking *one word at a time* rather than one sentence at a time. Now each improvisor has even less control of where the story is going.

Again in pairs, the improvisors will face each other and begin to tell a story based on a title suggestion give to them, pulling that title directly out of my ass. There are a couple of obstacles to having this exercise work successfully.

Two Things to Avoid

Firstly, the improvisors need to speak very clearly. Nothing grinds this exercise to a halt faster than one person having to stop everything to ask, "What?" Speaking clearly and directly at the other improvisor will help to overcome this potential stumbling block.

Secondly, a specific problem arises when the grammatical structure breaks down, with weird combinations of words arising that don't really make sense. The trick here is to just power through. The point of the exercise is not to create a perfect, grammatically correct treatise, so the occasional grammatical stumble is to be simply ignored is what that and for as just push on and don't worry about it. Like that.

Learning From The Mistake

But these stumbles can very well be an indication of one or both improvisors failing to *actively* listen to his/her partner. It often happens because one improvisor has slipped out of *the moment*, and is starting to anticipate where the sentence they are building is going. For example:

"I"
"am"
"going"
"to"
"the"
"store"
"where"
"are"
.... And here things suddenly stop.

What has probably happened is that one improvisor is anticipating something like "I am going to the store where *they sell ice-cream,*" while the second improvisor is anticipating, "I am going to the store.[period] Where *are* you *going*?" The unexpected addition of a verb after the *where* causes the first improvisor to stumble. It can happen even if you are *in the moment*, for sure, but with beginner improvisors it is often an indication that the improvisor has slipped back into some sort of pre-planning. The only thing to do when it does happen is to power through.

Again, after a few minutes of this glorious nonsense, one of the improvisors from each pair will summarize what their story was about. The whole point of the exercise is about discovering what it is like to let go of control. The improvisors need to be asked, and need to ask themselves: Were you able to let go of control? Was it fun to? Was it frustrating? What happened to the story because you could not steer it in a particular direction?

Letting Go Means Trading Off Control

Letting go of control is vital for successful improv. It does *not* mean that no one is in control, it just means that control, as demonstrated in both *Sentence at a Time* and *Word at a Time*, shifts back and forth from one improvisor to another. If an improvisor feels frustrated because the story did not go where he/she wanted, then I suggest that said improvisor needs to realign their paradigm of what *is* and *is not* frustrating, because, ultimately, this is what improv comedy is exactly about. Successful improvisors need to enjoy being taken into uncharted territory.

Exercise 5: Dr Know-It-All

This *Word at a Time* exercise is also a good beginner exercise because it is one that can actually be developed into a performance piece in a number of different ways. A favourite improv game is called *Dr. Know-It-All*, where a host asks questions of a single character, Dr. Know-It-All, who is made up of several improvisors and perhaps even an audience member, standing all together and acting as one individual. Dr. Know-It-All answers whatever questions are given him using the *one word at a time* technique. The inevitable absurdity of the answers is what makes this an audience favourite. Another possible use of *word at a time* is in a more traditional scene, but with two or more improvisors (usually standing very close together and linking arms) acting as a single character in the scene and saying the character's dialogue using *one word at a time*.

Everyone Shares the Glory

Just for fun, I want to give you an example of the worst possible example of an improvisor *not* letting go. After finishing the *Word at a Time* exercise, we began discussing it, and noting as a group the value of letting go of control, when one of the improvisors explained why their story had become so strange. He informed the other improvisor that she was, "supposed to say ____" but messed it up by saying something else. Boooo. Missed the point! She was not *supposed* to say anything other than what being *in the moment* made her say. When I reiterated this point to the first improvisor he argued, basically pointing fingers at the other improvisor for causing the activity to fail. I have four things in response to such an argument:

Firstly, having the story go crazy is not a fail, it is the expected outcome of this particular exercise.

Secondly, having a few stumbles is no big deal, especially when this is a training exercise.

Thirdly, *all* members are responsible for the success or failure of a scene. I know that sounds very unfair, because there are improvisors who are better and funnier than others... but thems the breaks: If a scene fails in front of an audience, you will feel what I mean; everyone in equal proportion walks off in the silence the audience dishes out. If the scene succeeds, the applause is directed at everyone, and you are free and welcome to soak up your equal portion of it. It is your job on stage to make the other improvisor look good, but we will get to that later.

And fourthly, don't argue with me.

Remember, in performance you cannot control what the other improvisors think, say, or do, and if you try, you need to stop immediately. If you can not stop, you need to get off stage and not come back until you can.

Now go to your room!

A WHOLE LOT OF NEGATIVE

Shooting For a Masterpiece

While the majority of improv exercises and 'scenes' for the beginner improvisor involve a *restriction* of some sort, and take the form of games, or as it is called in the business - *handles*, the ultimate goal of improv is to be able to create a scene, sketch, or even an entire play from scratch, right before the audience's eyes, without using *restrictions* or handles at all. Just get up on stage with no idea what you are going to say and create a *masterpiece of the theatre*. To be able to do this properly should be the end goal of anyone who is interested in a career in improv, at whatever level. And... go.

Correcting Bad Behaviour

But before you throw yourself onto stage to create that masterpiece, using *restriction* exercises is a good way to isolate particular potential problems, especially those that come from habitual behaviours that have developed through a lifetime of dealing with the great unwashed mass of stupidity that is society. As is true with dealing with any behavioural problem, the first step is *to recognize the problem. Restriction* exercises do this by revealing to us how often we want to resort back to some particular behaviour. Then, these same exercises offer us techniques to overcome this habitual tendency by giving us alternatives that are better suited for improv theatre.

Real Life Has Taught Us All Wrong!

Sometimes it's not easy. It is not easy for a number of reasons. Many of these *behavioural problems* have to do with things that we do naturally in 'real life' that may be very useful out there, helping us in some way to survive the endless drudgery of passing time that is our slow unfocused stumble toward the grave. But in the magnificent, more important, and ultimately more real world of improv, these self-same things that we use as *tools for survival* become *obstructions* that prevent us from succeeding on stage. They must be overcome, and if possible, destroyed. If you can obliterate them entirely, all the better.

The first of these behaviours that needs some serious behaviour-cide is *saying no*.

Just Don't Say No

No is very useful in the real world. As children it is probably the word that we hear most for many, many years. As your tongue inches toward the light-socket: *No*! As your hand reaches for the stove element: *No*! As you eye up the living-room wall, pen in hand: *No*! As you reach into the toilet bowl to grab your freshly plopped poop: *No*!

The Evil Power of No

Around age two we also discover that *no* has incredible power for us as well. We turn the tables on our parents and start throwing the word back at them. Go brush your teeth. *No*! Go to bed. *No*! Eat your vegetables. *No*!

Discovering the power of *no* is a moment of incredible awakening for us as young humans. *No* is used to control you (we first learn as a children), and then we can use it to control others! Sweet!

Saviour and Destroyer

No is a saviour and a protector. Get into the stranger's car. *No*! Time to go to piano lessons. *No*! Do you want to try this new food you have never tried before? No*!*

But *no* is a destroyer too. *No* is a fun-killer. Need proof? It was the *government* that came up with the *Just Say No* campaign. I rest my case.

She's a two-edged bitch, that *no*, and a weird mixed metaphor to boot.

Over-Using No

As we move toward adulthood we use *no* more and more. We use it to avoid all the things we have learned that we don't like, which is fair enough. But we start to overuse it. We start using *no* as a *stalling and protective mechanism* when confronted with anything new whatsoever. We also use it as a *default answer* for when we don't know what to say; better to say *no* than agree to something before you have had time to think about it. In the real world, that might be good thinking, but on stage it is wrong and evil and stupid and terrible and damaging and awful. But no judgment.

It is these uses of *no,* as a *stalling and protective mechanism* and as a *default answer,* that need to be recognized whenever it happens, and to be ultimately eliminated from your behaviour when performing improv.

How do you do this? *Don't say* no. Ever. Kinda...

No Good Reason

When watching an improv scene on stage, the most obvious amateur mistake that an improvisor can make is saying *no*. *No* stops everything. *No* slows everything down, often delaying the inevitable. *No* is often a judgment (and a negative one at that) of an idea offered by another improvisor on stage and as such destroys the teamwork. *No* rarely offers something new to the scene, and can be boring to watch. *No* can occasionally be so disruptive that it becomes an example of the dreaded *cringeworthy* (term © Drew McCreadie) that is as deadly to comedy as the plague, and needs to be avoided with equal zeal. (Ok, honestly, avoid the plague with more zeal.)

Get it? It is bad.

Good Examples of Bad

Here are some examples of exactly what I am talking about with some discussion on why saying *no* is not the best choice, and how saying something else (i.e. *YES*) as an alternative will take you to new and exciting places.

Example A. Blocking

Improvisor A: Well, here we are in Hawaii!
Improvisor B: No, we're not. This isn't Hawaii.

We start with the most rudimentary mistake; *Blocking* is saying *no* to another improvisor's idea. It is comedy death. It stops everything in its tracks.

The first improvisor in this example has suggested that they are in Hawaii. What a great place! What a great place for a scene! Think about all the great things that you can do in Hawaii! You can surf, and lie on the beach, or build a rocketship, or perform a forgotten ancient ritual, or grate cheese into a bowl, or teach a monkey to sing. It's like you can almost do anything there!

As an audience member I immediately start to see the beach and the palm trees laid out before me in my mind's eye. This is going to be great... What? Oh, they are not in Hawaii? Where are they? What should I do with the palm trees and beach my mind created? How long do I need to wait in this scene before the two improvisors can agree on where they are so I can join in by picturing it in my head?

And, me the audience member thinks, how could *Improvisor A* have made such a huge mistake by not recognizing that they were not actually in Hawaii? It's like something is going wrong, like this scene isn't working. I, and my fellow audience members are confused. We are starting to hate this, and hate these people on stage.

Blocking Undermines The Other Improvisor

Also, by saying *no, Improvisor B* has completely undermined Improvisor A, as if to say, "Hawaii? What a terrible stupid rotten idiotic talentless idea!" Not good for teamwork, which is what improv is.

And what will happen next? What will be the next line? Improvisor A is pretty much forced to address the fact that the two of them disagree as to where in the world they are standing. It would be pretty weird not to address that. So now how much of the scene is going to be about where they are? Unless the *entire* scene becomes about not knowing where they are, then they will eventually agree on where they are and start doing something. Well, get to it: do *that* something. If the something else is what the scene will be about, then let's see that!

(And please don't think that having an entire scene about not knowing where they are is original. Amateurs that have made this *blocking* mistake have turned many-a-scene into this. It's been done. A million times. Yawn.)

Example B. Stalling

> ***Improvisor A***: Ok boss, I've disabled the security system. Now let's see what's in this safe!
> ***Improvisor B***: No, wait. We need to check that we have all the right tools.

Why do we need to check for the tools? Just start opening the safe! I wanna see what is in the safe!! That sounded fun! Waiting to check to see what tools they have is... not fun.

This is a classic case of *stalling*. Again, if they end up having the correct tools then they will start breaking into the safe, so why not just start breaking into the safe? I wanna see what is inside that safe!!! But if they don't have the correct tools, then we may never see inside the safe. In this way, Improvisor B has blocked Improvisor A's idea of breaking into the safe, as if to say, "Nice idea about two crooks safe-cracking, but I have this way, way better idea about crooks that forget to bring the right tools, so let's stop doing your stupid idea and do my genius, way better idea."

Being Too Literal

Even if this *stalling* is not consciously done in this judgmental way, it may reveal another trap that beginner improvisors sometimes fall into, that *of being too literal.* Yes, it does actually make sense to check for the correct tools; if you were real safe-crackers then you might actually do that. But this is theatre, and we want it to be interesting and exciting. There is something called *artistic license* that allows us not to have to sit silently with the crooks in the car for the entire 45 minute drive over to the robbery site. We can join them as they start the robbery, and it is ok for us to assume they have checked their tools.

Beginner improvisors will do things like getting right down on the floor, out of the sightline of the entire audience, and therefore completely unseen, because in real life getting right down on the floor is what you would really have to do to do whatever they are doing. But now I can't see what you are doing, so it doesn't matter how realistic it is, whatever it is that you are doing that I can't see. You need to discover some less literal, less realistic way to do what you need to do so that I can see it.

To fix a car you need to open the hood, then turn on the portable work light, and then open your tool box and find the right wrench amongst all the others before you can undo the flux-capacitor or whatever the hell is in there. In improv, you just need to open the hood, the correct wrench is right there -- maybe already in your hand! Maybe the hood is already open. You don't *need* to turn the light on. Get to fixing the car!

I am not saying you should be totally unconcerned about depicting reality, or that adding specific details to your environment is not a good thing. In fact, good miming skills, and being specific about the physical world around you on stage is very important. Just don't let a desire to be true to life stop you from getting to the action of the scene.

Example C. Judging

> ***Improvisor A***: Hey Susie! It's your birthday. Wanna have a party?
> ***Improvisor B***: No, mom, let's go bowling.

Here is another case of saying *no,* which might not *technically* be a block because an alternative suggestion is offered that may forward the scene, and the previous line was given in the form of a question. But, to my mind, I would toss this one onto the *block* pile simply because no reason was offered as to why they shouldn't have a party, other than the implied reason that Susie would prefer to go bowling, which is pretty weak. Now, of course, it is very possible that a scene about Susie and her mom going bowling will be brilliant, *<u>but</u>* there is an *equal possibility* that a scene about Susie having a birthday party would be just as awesome. So why aren't we having the party? Now, it could be that the Susie character is a very hard-to-please kid that doesn't like anything, but does that mean that this scene will consist of her just rejecting a list of ideas offered by her mom? Hmm. I'd pass on buying a ticket to see that.

The idea of a party was on the table. Take it. It is a gift. Susie can still be a hard to please little whiner without saying no. "Yes, I want a party! A big one, with real dinosaurs!" Now mom has to try to put that together. Much more interesting than watching mom go through a list of suggestions just to have Susie reject them all.

Almost every case of saying *no* or *blocking* is, in part, a *judgment* by one improvisor upon the suggestion offered by the other. This *judgment* can come from various places, with varying levels of counter-productiveness. It might come from *habitual behaviour* and, as such, is pretty subconscious and innocuous as far as intent. It still needs to be exterminated.

Making a Judgment From Fear

But *judgment* can also come from a fear that you will have no good ideas related to the other improvisor's offer... you know nothing about Hawaii, and so you would prefer the scene happen in Denmark, which, because of a mix-up in scheduling during university where you ended up taking four semesters of Danish history, you accidently became an expert in. In this case, it is a deliberate attempt to negate the offer of the other improvisor and replace it with your own. You might not consider it a *judgment* because in your heart you know that Hawaii is just as good of an offer as Denmark, and you only wanted to change it because it would make things easier for you. But it *is* a form of *judgment* insofar as you are judging which suggestion will offer the best possible outcome. It is *judgment, pre-planning*, not being *in the moment*, and potentially immoral in some religions, who knows. At the very least, it is counter-productive as you simply cannot control all aspects of a scene. For various reasons, some discussed already and some teed up for discussion, *judgment* of this nature will always result in frustration, and must *never* be allowed to happen.

Check Your Ego At The Mimed Door

In the pettiest of cases, *judgment* can come from a place of ego, where you simply just want it to be your idea and not the other guy's idea, regardless of anything else. Do I need to say this is not good? I will anyway. Not good. Not only is this jerk behaviour, this insecurity will be seen by the audience, as I will discuss later, and they will dislike you for it. Insecurity is the opposite of comedy, remember? Do not allow yourself to be this person.

Example D. Protecting

> ***Improvisor A***: Captain, we need to attack the Buzznoid starship while their shields are down.
> ***Improvisor B***: No, it's too dangerous.

What's wrong in this example? you may ask. It kinda sounds like dialogue from any number of sci-fi shows, right? The answer is that maybe nothing is wrong. But maybe it is one of the same culprits we have seen before re-raising its blockhead. Depends what happens next.

But, what I would like to know is why Improvisor B said *no*. Was it just the habitual behaviour again? Or is it because *he doesn't know what to do next in the scene*? Or is it because *he has a 'better' idea*? Or is he just *playing the character of the cautious ship's captain*. We don't know, let's say.

But my point here is: What would be wrong with the Captain replying, "Yes, absolutely! How would we do that?" (*doesn't know what to do*), or, "Affirmative, I will beam myself over and sleep with all their women," (*has his own 'great' idea he wants to get out*), or "Indeed, as long as we can do it without upsetting them" (*cautious Captain*). Because of the pitfalls that come from saying *no*, just say *yes*. Your scene will move ahead. It *may* move ahead if you say *no*, but very often it doesn't. As in ***<u>VERY</u>*** often! (that's all caps, bold, underlined and italics, in case you didn't notice)!

Saying *no* as a way of *protecting* is something we do very naturally in the real world off of the stage. But, that world is an illusion! Only theatre is real!

Protecting is a way of begging the other improvisor to come up with the next thing to do. If you really don't know what to say or do next, say *yes*, and see how that simple act will move the scene forward far more elegantly than protecting yourself with a *no*.

Example E. Defaulting

> ***Improvisor A***: Hey, buddy. Want to do some naked skydiving?
> ***Improvisor B***: No!

Yes!! Yes you do! And we want to see it! I offer this up as an example of the *habitual behaviour* many of us have of defaulting to *no* when asked anything out of the ordinary. (Remember here that this is one *character* asking another *character*, not someone asking *you* if you want to go naked skydiving. This is your big chance to say yes!!! So say it!)

I Guess I Hate Nature and Honesty

But, as we often try to make art reflect life, there *is* something natural and honest to saying *no* to an offer to go naked skydiving. I still hate it. It is natural and honest because most of us would reply to this question exactly like that. But let me say this: Most of us would say *no* even if we <u>wanted</u> to do it and <u>ended up doing it anyway</u>! It goes something like this in real life:

> ***Bill***: Hey, wanna go skydiving this weekend?
> ***Larry***: What?! No!.... when...?
> ***Bill***: Sunday.
> ***Larry***: How much?
> ***Bill***: $110.
> ***Larry***: Hmm.

See? Larry's first response was *What?! No!,* even though he immediately started to show an interest in it, and may very well decide to do it. It's just what we do, we say *no* first. We should probably try to change that in real life too; I think it might make us all happier, but we definitely should change it on stage.

Yes is More Interesting

"Skydiving?! What?! Yeah! When..." is much more interesting on stage than the only *slightly* different, *"What?! No!.... when...?"*. People are drawn to the boldness of someone who says *yes* first, and asks questions later; you want the audience to be drawn to your character.

So, in short. Don't say *no*.

Yes, but...

Inevitably there will be someone who will take all this in about avoiding saying *no*, but who cannot resist starting down the road of: "Yes, but can't you *sometimes* say *no* if..." Sorry to interrupt you, hypothetical questioning person, but the answer is NO! ...and of course also, yes.

No Can Be The Right Thing To Say

Obviously there are times that saying *no* makes sense, and is, as we theatrey people might say, *true to the scene*. (So *'obviously'* in fact, that it is banal to spend much time on it.) Saying *no* may set up a conflict that becomes the driving force behind the narrative for the entire scene. It is possible to have the best scene ever performed in the history of theatre ever that's based on, and filled with a whole bucket-load of *no*. Yes. It is *possible*. Happy, hypothetical question-asker?

But No Is Problematic

But here is the problem: People (especially new improvisors) who want *permission* to say *no*, or who want recognition of the possibility that saying *no* is the right thing to say (as in the case of my interrupted hypothetical friend above), are often the *exact same* people who cannot accurately identify (and therefore avoid) situations where *no* is the dead wrong thing to say. It is these same people who frequently say *no* at the worst possible times on stage. If you are a seasoned, experienced, naturally brilliant, hysterical, improv genius, and working with a team of improvisors with whom you have worked for many years, then: a) why are you reading this book?; and b) yes, you can say *no* whenever the hell you feel it is the best thing to do. But for the rest of you, the answer is: no!

Yes is The Better Choice

Why we need to address the problems that saying *no* potentially poses is because, as I hope I have clearly expressed, saying *no* is so very, very, very frequently done subconsciously and habitually, and as a defense mechanism -- often as a way of protecting ourselves and our insecurities, or just plain stalling and wasting everyone's time. *Yes, almost always, is a better thing to say*. It adds to the scene, moves it forward.

Do Not Take It As A Challenge

Do not, as a beginning improvisor, take the "don't say no" *rule* on as a personal challenge wherein you will be the one beginning improvisor in history that will master saying *no* before learning how to master saying *yes.* Please don't be that guy! There are thousands of you already, and the demand for you is zero! Don't look for examples of when saying *no* worked to bring to our attention, because we professional improvisors already know that it *can*. It doesn't matter that it worked, because what you don't see when you point to an example of when saying *no* worked, is what *would have* happened if the improvisor had said *yes* instead. You also don't see, in the exceptional example, the gazillion instances of *no* revealing the panicked amateur who has forgotten one of the most fundamental and simplest *rules* of improv. Just say *yes.*

Now go to your room!

Exercise 6: Yes and...

Here is the classic improv exercise that addresses the problem of saying *no*. Used and perhaps overused, this exercise is so simple, and yet so revealing. It is the single best way to experientially come to terms with the power of *yes* as an alternative to *no*, and of experiencing how strong the natural propensity to say *no* as our first choice is for many of us.

The instructions are simple. Two improvisors will perform a scene, based on some suggestion as a starting off point, but they must begin *every line of dialogue* with, "Yes, and..."

MUST.

Every line!

"Yes, and..."

NOT "Yep, and..."

NOT "Yeah, and..."

NOT "Ok, and..."

NOT "Well.. yes, and..."

ONLY, "Yes, and..."

To fully get what this exercise can teach, you must stick to this very simple rule to an absolute *T*! If you allow yourself to veer off even a little bit, you slip, even subconsciously, into the world of trying to find ways to circumvent this simple instruction rather than really sinking down into it to glean its full lesson.

When doing this exercise with a group of new improvisors, I will *side coach*, which means sit off to the side, in my place of self-righteousness, and will yell out at them *"Yes, and..."* every time they fail to say exactly that. It is inevitable that I will need to do it several times.

You Will Want to Say No

What you will discover when doing this exercise is that you will want to say *no* often. You will also discover that the scene will go to unexpected places in part because the natural response of saying *no* is eliminated, and so the natural direction of the scene, i.e. the direction that might most likely align itself with what would naturally happen in reality, is also likewise eliminated. You will also find that the scene will be filled with a lot of energy, most of it positive, but potentially quite manic. I also consider this to be a good thing, as it is usually quite compelling and entertaining to watch.

And you will have a lot of fun.

You may also discover the fun that comes with knowing that your fellow improvisor *must* say yes to your offers, and then, in response, discover ways to deal with that.

> ***Sue***: *Yes, and* you should kiss me on the lips.
> ***Larry***: *Yes, and* one day I might.

You Can Always Say Yes

After doing this exercise, I remind improvisors that when doing any scene ever, they can, if they want, decide quietly to themselves to take on the *restriction* of this exercise, and just say, "Yes, and....".

In a scene (as opposed to an exercise) you can be a little more loose with the rule, allowing yourself to say something other than, "Yes, and..." occasionally as the scene demands. But peppering in a deliberate "Yes, and..." into a scene, especially when you are at a loss as to what to say, it a good step toward breaking the habit of saying *no* as your default.

If you are ever at a total loss for what to say, just say *yes* and see what happens. It's so easy. Just remember it. And do it, and your improvisation will take an immediate and noticeable leap forward in competency. It's that important!

SPECIFICALLY NOT NOTHING

Vagueness Is Kinda... You Know.

Let's start the discussion of the next important improv principle, that of being *specific*, with an example dialogue of an improvised scene that is *not* specific.

> *Two improvisors, a man (A) and a woman (B), take the stage. They are given the starting suggestion of "at the office". They begin their scene.*
>
> ***Improvisor A***: Hey.
>
> ***Improvisor B***: Hi.
>
> ***Improvisor A***: So, I got you something.
>
> ***Improvisor B***: Really? Wow! What is it?
>
> ***Improvisor A***: It's right here.

***Improvisor A** hands **Improvisor B** a (mimed) gift box.*

Improvisor B: Thank you.

She opens it. She looks pleasantly surprised to see what is inside.

Improvisor B: Oh my god! Thank you so much.

Improvisor A: You like it?

Improvisor B: Where did you get it?

Drew jumps off his seat of self-righteousness in the corner and storms the stage.

Drew: *What the hell is going on?!*

He beats both improvisors unconscious.

Ok. That last bit might not have happened, but the dialogue, did, many times, by many different improvisors. Although storming the stage and throwing the improvisors a beating didn't really happen... yet, my question remains valid: *What the hell is going on?*

The Common Beginner Mistake

After *blocking*, or saying *no*, this is the most common mistake of beginner improvisors and one of the mistakes that is the simplest to avoid; this scene lacked all sorts of *specificity*, and was filled with lots and lots of *vagueness*: We don't know who they are, we don't even know their names, we don't know their relationship to each other, we don't know where they are, we don't know what they are doing, and we don't know what he gave her.

What's In The Box?

All the other vagueness aside, let's start with the question that would most likely be on the forefront of the audience's collective mind, namely: *What's in the damn box?*!

The most likely reason why *Improvisor A* didn't say what is in the box, especially as a beginner improvisor, is quite simply that he doesn't know, so he ends up saying nothing; *Improvisor A* has no idea what he got *Improvisor B*, and he is hoping that she will think up something brilliant and funny that will make the scene.

When asked, *Improvisor A* might say that the reason he didn't know what he gave her was because *he couldn't think of anything*. Really? Couldn't think of *anything*? Anything?

It Is Impossible to Not Think of Anything

That is impossible! Because it is *mimed*, what he gave her could be *anything* in the universe: A diamond ring, a flower, Chinese coins with a square hole in the centre, a piece of cake with an icing panda, a WiFi router, a ceiling fan, a left shoe, vanishing cream, a lump of coal, an old key, a shifting tide, bed sheets, a stolen bicycle, a red clothes rack, a tissue, cowboy spurs, a empty box with an empty box inside, roasted cashews, a fork, a white tennis skirt, a Kinder Surprise toy, a table with table cloth, an blue shirt, some forest moss, children's socks, a bandana, a half-eaten banana, the hole from a guitar, an electricity bill from three months ago, a tooth filling, an embryo, a fighter jet, an apple wit a worm in it, a back brace, a blue feather, a red feather, a yellow feather, a green feather, an orange feather, a multi-coloured feather, a featherless bird, some seeds (maybe with magical properties), dried squid, a baby's first giggle, a towel, a bit of rope, his heart, his ear, a cup of homemade soup, a language CD, a warm coffee, some candy, a pirate's eye-patch, shards of the magic power crystal of the lost kingdom of Kalor-Nakhamitoo, some underwear, unclaimed glasses from lost and found, a photograph of mom and dad, a caulking gun, tickets to a Broadway show, magnetic silver balls, a planet mobile, money, a parrot, Victoria's actual secret, a sun visor, a gift basket of soaps and shampoos, a magic bean, a damaged door handle, a thimble, a light-bulb, a piece of paper, last year's report, crumpled up Christmas wrapping paper, her walking papers, a switch blade, a cork, cattle, a license plate, a stapler, lint from his navel, flea powder, a USB powered face-fan, a toenail clipper, toenail clippings, a battery, crispy pork, a compass, a hairnet, balloons, a screwdriver, a bottle of wine, a cute terrier puppy, an evil kitten, Satan's scepter, a bucket, a dinosaur egg, a regular egg, a slave, an alien, a judge's bench, the last chip in the bag, a piece of jade, glitter, skating lessons, venetian blinds for a dollhouse, whispers in the dark, flooring tiles, a hole into another dimension, a coupon for a back waxing, a tree, a stanchion, Airpods, a hairclip, tweezers, news about the promotion, a photograph of his mother swimming, scissors, King Arthur's sword, bubble wrap (already popped), a penny, a tuba, the Infinity Stones, a map of the Panama Canal, a special cloth for cleaning glasses, a treasure map, a bit of cardboard, melted ice-cream, an unidentifiable white powder, a piece of Swiss cheese with the holes filled in, passwords to every porn site on the internet, a bit of cotton, a carrot, a stool sample, a set of wrenches, a stone, a time machine, a piggy bank, a newspaper, a radio, a wallet he found on the street, a newspaper from the future, a crayon, a cable car ticket, a seashell that she sells by the seashore, a shotgun, a wall, a house, a car, a boat, a plane, a cigar, a bracelet with his name on it, a razor, a curse, a sheet of wax paper, a toothbrush, a waterslide, a World War Two relic, a bag of marbles, cannon fodder, a ball of mud, the answers to the test, seaweed, a widget, good morals, a handbag, an old man he found in the park, an Indiana Jones whip, a bottle cap, a whistle, a cup-o-noodle, the apple Eve ate from, a child's textbook, a soggy black plum, a ukulele, slippers, silly string in a can, a re-sealable plastic baggie, some tinsel, a condom, plans to the Deathstar, antiperspirant, a constellation, piano music, mints, a green M&M, a get out of jail free card, a single peanut, a kilo of cocaine, a stuffed toy, a rabid dog, their dead boss, a sex toy, an African drum, a can of tuna, proof of alien life, an old tire, membership into some offensive organization, a hammock, a pair of pants, a hammer, a Bluetooth remote camera shutter trigger, a cricket bat, the cutest cat photo in the history of photography, a laptop computer power cable, a necklace, some dominos, a birdwatcher's field guide, a shepherd's staff, a shepherd's pie, a shepherd, a pie, salt water, dad's porno magazines, a baby goat, a baby with a goat's beard, a brochure, a old TRS-80 computer, salt in bucket, a carpet, a CD, cold press Virgin olive oil, a torpedo, a television, a micro projector in a pen, a book, a drawing of himself as a bunny, a plot twist, a cell phone, the Holy Grail, a remote control for a old-time VCR, swizzle sticks, a thermometer, a lamp, three mice he blinded himself, a calendar, lice, Santa's hat, the new watch from Apple, a raincoat, an umbrella, an ice-cube, a lawn chair, a cape, a gondola, bad advice, a mug, unpopped popcorn, a door, a toilet, a painting, the next iPhone three months before it is released, lingerie for her, lingerie for him, brass knuckles, a sweater, a sewing machine, a brick from the house that the guy traded a red paperclip for, a stuffed teddy bear, a compilation of every time Joey entered a scene in Friends, a jar of cold cream heated to boiling hot, the latest microprocessor, the special collectors' edition re-mastered Led Zeppelin box set with never-before-heard out-take tracks, a knitting needle, a chip of stone from a castle wall in Germany, a radio antenna, peas, walnuts pained to look like animals, a call to arms, a bottle of Crown Royal with the cap missing, a toy elephant, suspenders, old coffee grounds, a bag of cookies, a machinegun from World War II found in an abandoned storage room, a tip on a horse race, a quark, a paperclip, a wish, an old chewed-up pencil, a cabbage, a bootleg DVD, a roofing tile, a pond, a bottle of sparking water, a shark's tooth, a morning-after pill, a horse, a gorilla suit, an external hard-drive, a porch for her house, a back-scratcher, oil stains, the empty net bag that onions come in, an inhaler, a half-drank bottle of water, a necklace of baby-teeth, pieces of a dried riverbed, a postcard from Romania, a candle, a vase, fake flowers, a street sign, a bad dream, a spaceship, a pole-vaulting pole, a controller for a video game system, some unverifiable facts, whip cream, a bag of cement, a crown, a flow chart that explains everything, blue-tooth enabled pajamas, divorce papers, a stiff drink, a taxi receipt, a mountain top, a fake I.D., tap dancing shoes, incriminating photos, a bomb with an old alarm clock as the timer, an iceberg, jelly beans flavoured like vomit and snot, some copper wire, a coffee-table book with pictures of every F1 race winner opening a bottle of Champaign, the antidote, a list of the best beaches in the world, a chain letter, a placemat, the first baseball card ever printed, a ribbon, a horseshoe, some sandpaper, a teapot (short, but not stout), a ball of earwax found unclaimed by the janitorial staff, a remote control drone, a Battlestar Galactica Viper pilot's helmet, a copy of this book (in fourth edition – with even more things added to this list, like rainbow pants, a Covid-mask, and floral earmuffs), an Olympic silver dollar coin set, a raisin, an original unopened copy of the first Beatles album on cassette tape, the ancient Egyptian symbol for life, grandma's teeth, a ticket to heaven, fireworks, an eraser, a gummy bear, guitar strings, an apple turnover, a bayonet, a cart, a ganglion, an evacuation order, a doorstop, a handicapped parking pass, an inflatable monkey, a jester's hat, a lost file, more paperwork, a pneumonic drill, myrrh, an electric guitar signed by Jimmy Page, a bank account, overalls, premade salsa, a quiet moment, re-gifted dishes, a storage tank, the name of the guy who sang that song that has been playing in her head for the last two weeks, unopened letters from the president, a large hunk of amethyst, a Japanese Oni ogre from myth, varicose veins, a well-oiled machine, opera glasses, yodeling lessons, the last page ripped from an adventure book, an abscess, a bum-deal, crispy pork on rice, credit with the mafia, damaged goods from the warehouse, a three ring-binder with a list of everything she has said to him for the past seven years, a collector plate, a miniature Marshall stack, the ax Abraham Lincoln used to cut down the cherry tree, an afterthought, a flashlight, a snake, a crutch, a trunk, a duffle-bag, long-johns from a stranger, chopsticks, a bowling trophy, a missing tile from Carcassonne, an engraving, a single blade of grass, perfume, the last bottle of Coke with actual cocaine in it, a deck of cards, a severed head, tear gas, a pickle, a straw, a hot potato, burnt toast, a haircut, a shoestring, a leaf, coupons clipped from a magazine for a better present (other than a back-waxing), a motorcycle helmet, some ants, a rash, a card he made himself, duct-tape, her name written out in ones and zeros, or even a spatula. To name a few. Anything.

Nothing Good

What the improvisor really means when he says he *couldn't think of anything* is that he couldn't think of anything '*good*', and so, said nothing instead. My mom used to tell me that *if you can't say anything good about someone, then you shouldn't say anything at all.* That is good advice in the real world, and will help to explain why I am not going to tell you what I think about these two improvisors. But this advice does not hold true in improv. *Anything* is better than nothing. Because nothing... is bad.

Anything Leads to Something

Absolutely any one of the suggestions I listed, or any other idea that could have been dreamt up is better than leaving it up to the other improvisor to say something. A diamond ring or flowers is a great idea; it is something that a man might actually give a woman, and therefore would ring true, and would be a great start to a scene about an office romance. A membership into an offensive organization would be a great starting place for a bit of conflict in a scene as she tries to refuse the gift, as would lint from his navel. An iceberg or a hole into another dimension would take the scene into the world of the very weird, which would be amazing to watch and see where that goes. Plans to the Deathstar would have taken the 'office' that was their original suggestion into an office setting quite different than 'the office' that the audience member who made the suggestion probably imagined. Even something more pedestrian, like a fork or a raincoat, would allow for any number of possible responses from Improvisor B as she explains why she is so delighted by the gift. And at the very least she would have *something* to talk about. Anything is a good idea... except nothing.

Cut Yourself Some Slack

It is impossible *not to think of anything* if we disregard our instinct to want to say something *good.* Without judgment and self-censorship ideas will flow like... I don't know... something... wet... like... uhmm... flowy... what you call it... liquid.. clear... you can drink it... ah... I can't think of it, but you know what I mean.

What stops us from saying something is the *judging* we are doing. Remember that judging is not being *in the moment,* it is being in the future, worried about what people will think of your suggestion, and/or where you will be able to take the idea after you release it from your mind onto the stage. Get back in the now! Just say something. It'll be good!

You Are Boring, Obvious and Stupid

Perhaps you might argue that, ok, you understand what I mean, but still, you watch other improvisors and the ideas they come up with are so interesting and brilliant and unique and unexpected, while your ideas are always so obvious and stupid. You would never have thought of *plans for the Deathstar,* as something that you might give a fellow office worker. The first thing that popped into your brain was a *coffee* because that is what you actually would give someone at the office. Boring. Obvious. Stupid.

Ok. I hear you. And I get it. The answer to that is this: that *coffee* is <u>way</u> better than vaguely handing another improvisor something unspecific and hoping they come up with something good. Better, period! Better, always. Period.

The more you practice being *in the moment*, and the more you allow yourself to just say whatever, the more varied your ideas will become. *Tangential associations* will begin to reveal themselves to your semi-sub-consciousness. It does take time for your brain to get over the self-censorship that it has been trained to do for the majority of your life. If you stay with it, you will one day surprise yourself with a super-weird, super-excellent idea. Or you will die first, and then it doesn't matter.

Who Is Responsible For Filling The Box?

So whose job is it to say what is in the box? In theory, it is everyone on stage's responsibility to build the reality of the scene for the audience. In practice, it is the responsibility of whoever can do it fastest, and that usually mean the first one to speak.

"Here, I got you this box of Legos." is perfect, and is, *by far* the best way to go as the improvisor who came up with the idea is being specific about what it is. "Here I got you this," followed by: "Wow, a box of Legos," also works, but *only* works because the second improvisor picked up the dropped ball of the first and didn't engage vagueness herself. It is a little unfair as the first improvisor is putting the responsibility to come up with the idea on the other improvisor. But they are a team, and dropped balls do sometimes happen, so as a team they were successful. What doesn't work, as in our example earlier, is when there is even a single line of extra dialogue before we find out what is in the box, when neither improvisor picks up the ball and stalls with vagueness.

A *ball* would also be a good suggestion for what is in the box.

Avoid Blind Offers

As a beginning improvisor, you must actively avoid *ever* giving what we call *blind offers*, that is "Hey! Look at *that*." Always be specific; either say what something is, or what you are doing, or mime it clearly enough that it is obvious to everyone. Never leave it up to your fellow improvisors, or I will throw you a beating.

Exercise 7: I Got You This

There is an exercise that can offer opportunity to practice being *specific*, while at the same time allowing a weird experiential understanding of how discombobulating *blind offers* can be.

The improvisors stand in a circle. In turn, starting with Improvisor 1 and moving around the circle, the first improvisor mimes handing something to the next improvisor in the circle. Try to mime something specific, i.e. what it is like to hand someone a bottle of wine as opposed to what it is like to hand someone a huge blob of slime. The first improvisor gives the blind offer line, "Here, I got you *this*." The second improvisor mimes taking the gift and then must *instantly* identify what the gift is, with a line like, "Nice! A bottle of wine!" or "What? Some radioactive slime?" No pausing! No pre-planning. See what is being mimed and say the first thing that pops to mind! If it is not clear what is being minded, say the first thing that pops to mind anyway.

This second improvisor then turns to the next improvisor and mimes handing this improvisor something completely different, again with the blind offer line, "Here, I got you *this*." And so it continues. This exercise needs to go on long enough that all the obvious mimes are used up and people start digging deeper to come up with new sizes and shapes and textures of things to hand to people.

Mime as Best You Can

What you may learn from this exercise is how unclear your mime is. You hand someone what you think is an obviously mimed *bottle of wine*, and they thank you for the *kitten*. They are not wrong! Because you are using the blind offer line, "I got you *this*" the second improvisor is being given the responsibility to come up with what the object is. It *is* a kitten, not a bottle of wine, no matter how 'good' your miming was. If you want it to be a bottle of wine, you need to really make the mime clear, or say it is a bottle of wine (which of course you are not instructed to do in this particular exercise). And once the other improvisor says it is a kitten, that's what it is. To resist this would be to *block*, and we've already gone over that.

Feel the Pressure

The improvisors will also likely feel the pressure of having to come up with the idea on the spot. Consider how unfair it is to have someone mime handing you something weird and now it is up to you to come up with what it is. Understand how it puts you on the spot. Feel the sweat building on your brow, and the panic as you try to guess at what this could possibly be. Experience how you wish they handed you something much more specific rather than that average size anything-could-be-inside box, and suffer through and commit to memory how unpleasant it is: now remember that, and don't do it to others in a scene. Be specific, don't leave it up to others, and be as generous and helpful in a scene as possible.

In short, in a scene never say, "I got you *this*!"

WHO WHERE & WHAT

We Need It

We need *specificity*! The improvisors need it, and the audience needs it. Without *specificity* a scene becomes, you know, like one of those things, like what-do-you-call it, like whatever; it doesn't have any of that thing that gives you the stuff you need.

We, *the audience*, need to know what's in the box. That is what everyone wants to know. Everyone! There is not one single person in the audience who is sitting watching and enjoying how clearly *Improvisor A* speaks, or how well *Improvisor B* is able to act, until we know what is happening. No one, except maybe your mom.

The Joyless Life of The Audience

We can't enjoy the scene, we can't even *see* the scene until we know what is going on. Remember, in improv, often everything is being mimed. There is no office, there is no desk with stacks of overdue reports, there is no water cooler, and there is no gift box. There is none of that until it is shown to us. These characters are not actually wearing business suits, or armor, or bikinis or anything until we *know* what they are wearing, then and only then can we imagine it. We need the *specificity* to see what is happening. And we need it *now.*

In particular we need to know three basic things about what is happening on stage. The more we know the better we can see, understand and enjoy what is happening. We need to know *who these people are, where they are,* and *what they are doing.*

We may not need to be told directly, but we need to be given enough hints and clues to figure it out. The smallest clue may be enough for us to start to imagine, but the more *specific* it is, the better it is for the audience, and, as I hope to show, for the improvisors as well.

Get Ready For Magic

By clearly defining in your head *who* you are, *where* you are and *what* you are doing, and relaying this information to the audience and your fellow improvisor as *quickly* and *specifically* as possible, you will discover that the *character* you are playing, the *environment* you are in, and the *actions* you are doing will take over, and give you all the things you need to do and say in the scene. It's magical! (or simple math, not sure.)

Let Your Body Do It For You

The simplest example: you will automatically open the door before you walk through it if the location of the door is clear in your own head. It will just happen. As long as the improvisor remember miming a door over there, every time he or she go there he or she will open the door (unless it was left open last time.) The same is true for how a character will respond, or what he/she will say, if it is clear who that character is. And an improvisor's body will just do the right motions if he or she is clear and specific about what he or she is doing. Think: *I am building something,* and your hands and arms may just flap around generally. Think: *I am building a tiny model tower out of toothpicks,* and your whole posture will change and you will instinctively lean in and delicately mime moving tiny things with great precision. You won't even have to think about it.

Having it specific in the improvisors' own heads is very important, but of course, they need to relay what they are thinking as quickly as possible to their fellow improvisors. That can be the tricky part, and I will discuss an exercise to help with that shortly.

Who

The first and most important thing we need to know is *who* the characters on stage are. It is my belief that this is the single most important thing that needs to be defined, and that the *where* and *what* are simply supporting of, and subordinate to, the *who*. Not everyone will agree with me on that, but *who* the hell are they? – See? The *who* is important!

Theatre Is About Character

All theatre is about *the characters*: what *the characters* did and/or what happened to *the characters*. Until we know who the characters are, we can't care. At the very least we need to know who they are in relation to each other. Do they know each other? What is their relationship and status in relation to each other?

There's Lots We Can Know

There are lots of things that we can know about a character. We can know their name, their race, their job, their marital status, their age (specifically or generally), their relationship to the other characters on stage, their mental and physical health, their desires, ambitions, wants or objectives, their fears and dislikes, their appearance and some indication of their moral fiber. We don't need to know all of it, but the more we know the better. Some of this can be revealed by dialogue, some by acting, by posture, and other elements by movement. In improv, much of what we learn about one character may come from the other improvisor, and how they react to, or what they say about the character.

An improvisor needs to be as specific as possible while balancing the flow and reality of the scene, and the amount of time and effort it will take to reveal character traits, against what the audience needs to know for them to feel they know enough. A scene of a guy buying a coffee at the coffee shop probably doesn't require the audience knowing what his mother's maiden name is.

Define Who You Are Or Someone Else Will

The *audience* needs to know *who the characters are,* but the *other improvisors* need to know as well. If you don't make it clear who you are, be prepared for another improvisor to define it for you. If you don't want to play the entire scene as the mute, tap-dancing, foreign cousin, then you better make it clear who you are before someone else defines your role for you, because once they call you *Mute Dancing Pedro*, that's who you are. An improvisor need to let everyone in on what he or she is thinking as quickly as possible, or the other improvisors and the audience will start making up their own interpretations.

All theatre requires the performer to know in their head who the character is that they are playing. Improv differs from other forms of acting because, without a pre-planned script, the other *performers* on stage don't know who the other improvisors are playing are until they are told. It is true that in a play, *Character A* may have no idea who *Character B* is until they meet as part of the story, but *Actor A* does know who *Actor B* is playing (because they have both read the script). In improv, that is not the case.

Clarity Will Activate Your Imagination

The more clear *who* the character is, the better the scene will be, and, almost more importantly, the easier it will be for the improvisors imagination take the character where it needs to go. The clearer *who* the character is, the easier and faster it will be to determine what the character will do given whatever might happen in the scene. It's almost as if the character reacts, rather than the improvisor. I know that sounds very artsy, but, it is true.

Be More Than Your Job

Sometimes *who* the character is, is very strongly tied to *what* the character is, i.e. he is the plumber, she is the Captain, he is grandpa, she is the burglar. Often that is enough for a scene to develop, true. But, I contend, if more is added, if the character is filled out a bit more, then not only has *a more interesting stage-picture* being created for the audience, more importantly the improvisor has made it easier to know what the *character* will say or do next.

Here is what I mean: So, an improvisor is on stage, and says, "I got here as quickly as I could." The other improvisor says, "Thank goodness! The toilet is backed up and I have guests coming over." It is pretty clear that she is endowing the first improvisor as the plumber, even though she has not said as much directly. The first improvisor could, of course, decide to be someone other than the plumber, the best she could find on short notice, like the local dentist who has agreed to come over and use his 'extracting skills' and do what he can to unplug her toilet. Because she has not *specifically* called him a plumber, the first improvisor is free to be whatever he want as long as he doesn't undermine what has already been *specifically* established. But, let's assume, for this example, he pick up what she is putting down and adopt the role of the plumber on an emergency call.

He could jump right into the problem and discover something (hopefully interesting and hilarious) as the cause of the toilet problem, adding nothing more to the character. *Or*, he could be the *squeamish plumber*, or the *plumber who is afraid of water*, or the *plumber that always makes inappropriate passes* at all his customers, or the *plumber that failed plumbing school*, or any number of modifiers to his plumbingness. By doing so, he will have given a second dimension to his character immediately, something to differentiate him from the other characters on stage, say, the second plumber that shows up. He have also given himself, the *improvisor* inside the *character*, a place from which the plumber's reactions originate. A *squeamish plumber* will just naturally behave very differently than a super-macho, medal-winning, *war veteran plumber.*

The more specific you are about who you are, the more you are who you will specifically be.

Three times fast, please.

Where

We also need to know *where* the characters are. The more *specific* it is, the clearer the picture becomes for the audience. At the office is a good start, but *where* in the office? What kind of office is it? Adding these details will help everyone.

Where Can Help Shape Who and What

In the plumber example of the previous section, knowing what kind of house our female character lives in will possibly have a huge effect on *what* happens, and may help to define *who* she is.

The scene would probably be very different if she lives in a huge mansion, a tiny little house with the bathroom right next to the dining room, or a new-age enviro-house that is carbon-neutral and made from wheatgrass and unicorn sprinkles. Knowing where she lives helps define who she is.

Everybody Needs To Be In The Same Place

But the simplest reason why you need to be specific about where you are, is so that everyone on stage is in the *same place.*

Picture two improvisors on stage, one is digging while the other, taking the role of supervisor, encourages the other to work faster.

> "Dig! Dig!"
> "I am trying, sir"
> "You need to finish this before nightfall"
> "My hands are all bloody, sir, and I can't feel my legs!"
> "I don't care. Keep digging!"

I stop the scene and ask the improvisors where are they? One says they are in ancient Egypt, building the pyramids, while the other thinks they are in a cemetery in England, digging a grave. With the improvisors unable to agree on where they are, how can the audience be expected to picture the scene? The audience doesn't know what is going on!!! And unless they find out *FAST* they will not care at all. Sooner or later one of the improvisors might say something that identifies it for us (*"The pharaoh is coming!"*), but until that happens the audience is lost. That's 5 or 6 lines of dialogue and no one, not even the *improvisors in the scene*, know where we are? How can that be good? Can't.

Simple Things To Help Establish Locale

What this scene needed was some *specificity*. While it was clear from the action of the scene that these characters were probably *outside* (although they could have been in a basement or dungeon somewhere), *outside*, in this case, this was not enough. A quickly line like, "Cemeteries make me nervous" would have been enough to let Improvisor B know that they are not building the pyramids.

A scene with two farmers in a field arguing about if it will rain might not require us to know what kind of crops they are growing, or what country they are in. Being *outside* in this case might be good enough. But *by* knowing what kind of crop it is, the picture becomes a bit clearer, and the two improvisors may gain some sort of inspiration from the *specificity*; being in a wheat field may take the imagination in a slightly different direction than being in a field of pineapples. It certainly looks different in the mind's eye of your audience. So although it is not needed, the extra specificity is always welcome and always a benefit to the scene.

Help Us Make The Right Assumptions

At the very absolute least, we all must be able to assume where the action is taking place. If a dentist is talking to his patient, then we can assume we are in a dentist's office unless we hear or see something that contradicts this. But two guys talking about the game, or two girls talking about the cute new guy at school, could happen anywhere. Don't just assume the audience knows what you are thinking. Someone should take a split second to say or do something that helps us, the audience, and the other improvisors, to have some clue as to where the action is taking place. The guy orders another beer from an imaginary mimed waitress. Bang: *They are at the pub.* The girls fiddle with the locks on their locker doors as they discuss. Presto: *They are at school*. And bada-bing, you will find that the audience is along for the ride with you much more eagerly.

What

What the characters are doing is also, obviously, very important. And my big tip here is: *do something*! *Talking about* _____ doesn't count. *Do* something *while* you are talking; perhaps not something that distracts from the talking. But I promise you, scenes with improvisors actively doing something, *anything*, is almost always more interesting than scenes with two improvisors standing and discussing something, no matter how interesting the discussion may be.

That does not mean that you can't be still in a scene, but if you are being still, *be still for a reason*. People love that! Be *actively still*, not still because you forgot to move.

Something Must Be Happening

A scene is best when there are *two things going on* simultaneously, one *external* and one *internal*. By *external* I mean, active, as in an actual movement of some sort. By *internal* I mean some kind of emotional or intellectual *struggle*, *awakening*, or *unleashing* that is happening within one or more of the characters. This is perhaps beyond the scope of this book, so suffice it to say that if two things are what I think you should be shooting for, then doing at least one thing is absolutely necessary.

And *do it*, don't *discuss it*, and *never* find reasons not to get at the problem directly. You can discuss while you are doing, but get *doing* it immediately.

In the plumber example from the previous section, after it has quickly (two lines) been established who these characters are, and what they are doing (namely fixing a toilet), *get right to it*. As the plumber is saying his next line, he should be opening the lid and having a look, or putting down his toolbox and taking out a toilet de-pluginator, or putting on his protective plumbing suit. What should never happen is a description of what you are going to do first. "Ok. Just let me put on my protective suit and then I'll have a look," *followed* by the action. Describe it as you do it, if you must. "Ok, I'm just putting on my protective suit," as he mimes it. "And let's take a look," as he looks into the bowl.

Never stand talking. That doesn't count as doing. Do something physically and you will discover how much easier it is to tap into your imagination.

Define it Quickly

An improvisor having a great idea of *who*, *what*, and *where* in her head is a great start, but of course she needs to relay that to the audience and the other improvisors too. She need to do this as *quickly* and *efficiently* as she can. Especially in the *Barprov* setting, the specifics needed for the scene to be imaginable for the audience need to be introduced instantly. In a practical sense, that means within the first four or five lines of the scene.

A Little Reveals a Lot

There are many techniques to revealing specific details, many of which will be discover with practice thing ***Who Where What*** exercise that follows. A simple and easy one is to call someone by name. A name can reveal a lot about a person. Calling someone Jim is different from referring to them as James, or Mr. Smith. A character named Bubba might instantly inspire different things than a character named Mr. Butterworth III.

An Example

By adding as much *specificity* as is possible, as quickly as is possible, a potentially run-of-the-mill scene has a better chance of blossoming into something quite unique. Consider our plumber example again, but with a bit of *specificity* added to each line. In the chart to the right I have listed what was revealed to the audience by the line.

"Princess Bucklebee, I came as quickly as I could!"	Her name. Some possible indication of her nationality. Her status in society: royalty. There is some kind of emergency. Some insight into their relationship: he comes when she calls.
"Thank goodness you are here, Mr. Johannes."	His name. Some insight into their relationship, quite formal or business-like, as she addresses him by his last name. Maybe some indication of his nationality.

"*Anything* for you, Princess."	Insight into their relationship. He is very dutiful, or perhaps has romantic interest? They have met before.
"My toilet is plugged and you are the only plumber who was open."	What is going on, the nature of the problem. Where they are: her house. His profession. Her level of desperation (she has tried other plumbers).
"I never close because I never sleep."	Insight into his character. He is a super-plumber, or he is a blowhard, or he has a sleeping disorder. Or a combination of the three.
"I have the ladies' group over for Sunday's erotic book reading in ten minutes!"	Insight into her character: hosts ladies' parties, but they are perhaps a bit naughty. Her panic about the toilet reveals she is very concerned about what others might think.
"Well, I spent sixteen years in a POW camp, so unplugging this toilet will be nothing compared to the torture and torment I went through."	Insight into his character: tough, can endure a lot, or perhaps he will have some deep psychological problems from his time in internment.

	Has a military background.
He is suddenly startled. "Oh my god! The Horror! The Horror!" He drops to his knees and weeps like a child.	Insight into this character: Despite his background he is easily disturbed.

By adding a little bit of *specificity* with each line, a deeper, more interesting story emerges than just a woman with a blocked toilet.

Note how much can be revealed by a single line. The first line told us a lot about both characters and the nature of the situation, before we even knew what the situation is! Throw in a single detail and it can have a huge consequence on the rest of the scene.

Be mindful and try to add a little bit of *specificity* to each line of dialogue and watch in amazement what the tiniest seed of an idea can grow into.

Exercise 8: Who Where What

To be able to supply *specificity* easily and quickly, only takes focus and practice. The ideas don't need to be 'good' or 'funny' they only need to be *specific*, especially at first.

Here is a simple exercise for building techniques for adding *specificity* to a scene. It involves two improvisors taking the stage. They are given a suggestion as a starting off point, one that they *must* utilize somehow in the scene. This suggestion is best if it takes the form of a simple *noun* (screwdriver, duck, boat) or a simple *adjective* (furry, brown, slippery) and not something from which a solid assumption of who, what or where can be made (a location (like a police station), for example, is not suitable for this exercise.)

How Long It Takes To Relate The Information

And so the scene begins. The goal of the scene is to see how many lines of dialogue it takes before everyone in the audience (of other improvisors) can answer the questions *who, what* and *where*. As soon as all three questions can be answered to some degree, the scene stops. In any case, the scene stops after 8 lines of dialogue. After each one of these short scene beginnings, the group goes over what *is* known about the *character*, the *location* and the *action*.

Repeat Until the Number of Line Decreases

This is done many times, discussing each time what managed to be revealed either through dialogue, acting, miming, movement or what-have-you. It is valuable to list all the things that were established, and how it happened, as sometimes improvisors are unaware of what they did, even when they did something right. Improvisors will discover that the smallest, simplest things are important in establishing details for the audience. It is also interesting to discover how adept an audience is at picking up subtle clues. More on that later.

Give Yourself Only Three Lines

Once all improvisors have managed to get to a place where all three things are being consistently revealed, limit the number of lines to three, rinse, and repeat.

This is one of those exercises that needs to be done over and over. It builds technique as improvisors discover various ways to introduce specific details to the story without being too obvious about what they are doing. But for now, don't worry about being obvious; being clunky and obvious, "Hello, neighbour who is a female dentist and older than me", is better than being vague, especially in this exercise (but less so in performance). Subtly will develop over time.

Quick and Simple

It is simple, without much effort, to be able to define two things with a *single line*. Keeping it quick and simple is the key.

"You called for a plumber?" He is the plumber. The scene is happening at the other character's place (home, office etc. we don't know yet.)

"Hey Steve, mom said you might be here in the garage." Our speaker and Steve are brothers. Steve is a male. Steve is the brother. They are in the garage. He has been looking for Steve.

"Doctor, will this hurt? This is my first cavity." The improvisor is a dentistry patient. The other improvisor is the dentist. They are probably in the dentistry office.

So as you can see, with a simple name or title, and/or some phrase like, *Dear*, *Honey*, *Sir*, *Madame*, *Buddy*, *Yo Bitch*, or *You there*, one can start to define the characters and the relationships. Some simple dialogue or a bit of mime or acting can help to establish other character traits, like age, or gender, as well as defining, or beginning to define, the activity and/or the location.

Don't Define All Three

Improvisors must be careful, in zealousness to be *specific,* that they don't go too far. I would highly recommend limiting each improvisor to personally establishing *only one or two* of either *who*, *where* or *what*. By establishing three all by oneself, an improvisor is starting to drive the scene and may even be guilty of *steamrolling*, which no one wants to do. If one improvisor defines all three, *who, where, and what* for a scene, they have told the other improvisor *who* he is, *where* he is and *what* he is doing. Of course a seasoned improvisor can take that and use it, but as a beginner it is very dangerous, and is often a result of a panicked, over-compensation. Take for example the following lines:

> *Captain, the aliens have taken over the bridge! We need to open the crystal chamber here in the engine room to neutralize their power beam.*

I think perhaps this improvisor has said too much. The second improvisor is now forced to play the Captain, and at the very least address this idea of opening the crystal chamber. This improvisor has also even specifically located the action within the spaceship, in the engine room.

It might better serve the scene for the first improvisor to have stopped with:

Captain, the aliens have taken over the bridge!

He has established that the other improvisor is the Captain, and that he is some sort of subordinate, the language suggests a ship, aliens suggests a spaceship. And a problem has already been introduced, namely the aliens on the bridge. Leaving it up to the other improvisor to establish *where they are*, or *what they are going to have to do* to solve the situation is far superior to having one improvisor lay it all out for us.

What to do If Someone Defines Everything

But it will happen where one improvisor drives the scene a little too far, and starts to let everyone else know who they are, where they are, what they are doing, what the problem is, and what the solution needs to be. It happens less and less with more seasoned improvisors. This is one of the most telling signs of an inexperienced improvisor.

If someone does end up defining all three things (and then some), the other improvisor must *immediately* add something else or may become *trapped in the first improvisor's idea*. Consider a plumber example again. "*Oh my god, thank goodness! The plumber! My toilet is plugged and I am hosting a party and my boss is here. You need to unplug the toilet and sneak out this window before anyone sees you.*" A lot has been established. If not careful, this scene will become the brainchild of one improvisor alone, and that is not the nature of improv. To avoid this happening, the second improvisor must now *introduce* something *immediately* so as to re-establish the scene as a two person endeavour. *"Well, this will give me a good chance to use my rodeo clown skills."* OR *"I am so thrilled to meet you! I am a huge fan of your, 'Adopt All of Africa Program'."* OR *"I just had an operation and I can't use my hands. You will have to be my assistant."* OR *"I no speak English good, I only speak coarse stereotype."*

It's a Gift

This is not a "*screw you, you can not contain me*", to the other improvisors; it is a *gift to them*. The other improvisor doesn't want to be trapped inside her own idea either; she is probably eagerly waiting and looking for some inspiration outside her own head to move the scene forward and in a different and unexpected direction. Improvisors who really *do* want the scene to come almost exclusively from their own imaginations, don't last long, and will soon be gone, as they will find themselves constantly fighting the true nature of improv which is the opposite of their desire. With beginners, the tendency to define too much comes from nervousness, anxiety, and a lack of trust (which may be well founded) that the other improvisors will not pick up the *specificity* ball as needed. The cure to this is to chill out, relax, and trust more. Simple.

Obviously, what an improvisor adds to avoid becoming trapped cannot undermine or contradict what has already been *specifically* established. Whatever is added should help to make the other improvisor look good.

MAKING THE OTHER GUY LOOK GOOD

Selflessness for Profit

One of the things I absolutely love about improv is that it is one of the rare times in life where altruism is self-serving. *Improv works best when everyone on stage is doing their utmost to make everyone else on stage look good.* If you can set up a fellow improvisor for a killer punch-line, everybody wins, including you. The fact that you teed up that killer line does not go unnoticed, and although someone else might have said the line that got the laugh, the audience is fully aware of the awesomeness of the teamwork, and are astonished by your ability to set it up. Conversely, improvisors who try to steal the show do stand out, but not in the way they hoped; the very nature of improv is self-correcting in this way, as the audience can see through this behaviour, and are unimpressed by this improvisor's failure to sync seamlessly with the rest of the team.

And what could be better than being on stage with other people who see it as their responsibility to make you a star?!

I know this sounds like I am prepping for a feel-good group-hug, but it's better than that: It's like group sex, in front of people, who are applauding you! (I assume, as I have never been applauded by strangers during group sex.)

Exploding Audience's Minds

One of the thrills for the audience is to watch the well-oiled machine of a highly functioning improv group. Audience members minds are blown to smithereens by how effortlessly improvisors seem to be able to do the impossible; it is like they are watching people who can read each other's minds. It is truly magical, and like all magic, it is based on a few simple tricks that make the seemingly impossible, possible.

If you want to really blow people's minds (and why wouldn't you?), here are some things you can do to make the other guy (or gal) look good.

Have Fun

Enjoy yourself on stage. Enjoy your time with others on stage and they will enjoy their time with you. As a beginner improvisor it may be difficult to get past all the things to remember, and all the non-thinking and non-judging that should be going on calmly inside one's panicked head, but don't forget to have fun. Fun is contagious, and we want the whole room infected. Enjoy fellow improvisor's work.

I have been fortunate enough to perform with the very best improvisors in Canada, which are some of the best improvisors in the world. I really enjoy their work, and have a load of fun being on stage with them. They make me laugh, a lot! Hopefully it is mutual, but even if it is not, I win, 'cause I got to perform with them!

Set Your Fellow Improvisors Up For Success

Whatever you do on stage, in the back of your mind leave room for the idea that whatever you do should set your fellow improvisor up for success. Give them your best ideas, allow them the leeway they need to do what they need, offer your support in the scene in any way you can.

If you know they can sing, and an opportunity to sing comes up, hand it to them. Likewise if they can dance, or do a great Argentinean accent, or can rap like a gangsta, allow them to do it.

And of course, don't set them up for failure. It might seem funny to put them in the hot-seat, trying to make them do something they can't, but don't leave fellow improvisors hanging high and dry.

Don't Just Accept, Embrace

To really make the most of your time on stage, don't just accept offers from fellow improvisors, *embrace* them. Recognize any offer as a gift, a bit of inspiration that you can riff off of, something that will add to the scene, and something that you didn't have to come up with yourself!

If a fellow improvisor makes an offer, adding something to the scene, do your best to figure out what they mean. Why did they introduce that specifically? What could they be getting at? When you guess it right, or the other improvisor sees what you think they were thinking and accepts this, you will hear the pop in the audience as the top of their heads blow off. Sometimes synchronicity just happens, but often you will need to coerce it a bit with a little concentration and mental effort. *Active listening*!

Add, Don't Edit

Make sure what is being added to a scene is not dismantling what someone else has built. Add to the story, don't edit it. Be very mindful never to undermine fellow improvisor or what has established in the scene. Trying to get the audience on your side at the expense of your fellow improvisors can backfire.

Dismissiveness

Be careful with dismissive characters. There is a subtle but significant difference between a *high status character* (the boss, the lord of the manor, a princess, the chief, the leader of the gang, the smart guy, the rich gal, etc.) and a *dismissive character*. Often in life, high status people can be dismissive, but resist the urge to play this high status character trait. Picture a scene with a snooty rich woman sitting in a café. The waiter comes to take her order, "Would you like something to drink?" True to character (but bad for improv) she dismisses him with a hand wave, like he is a piece of dirt. So he just leaves the stage. Now she is on stage by herself. Now what?

Two character traits that exist in real life but are very difficult to play on stage are *dismissiveness*, and *boredom*. Instead of *dismissive*, try *abusive*, and instead of *bored*, try a character that *hates* whatever 'bores' him. In the example above, this snooty rich woman could have been very abusive to the waiter, making all sorts of unreasonable demands, which would have established her high status... and we would have a scene rather than her just sitting on stage by herself. A high school kid who is 'bored' is boring to watch. A high school kid who absolutely *hates* having to spend any time in school is far more interesting.

Listen

Listen. Listen. Listen.

RACY BITS

Sexuality, Race, and Vulgarity

All forms of comedy will inevitably end up coming face to face with the problem of dealing with a topic, or using language that is not suitable, appropriate or acceptable to certain groups. Because of the improvised nature of improv, i.e. it is improvisation, these issues can come up more frequently because it is impossible to plan around it, and this offers challenges that are particular to this art-form.

'Objectionable' material usually falls into one of several categories. Vulgar or profane (my favourite), sexual (also my favourite), taboo topics (rape, child abuse, incest – not so favoured), hot-button (like politics, abortion rights, religion, or any of those things you are not supposed to discuss in polite company – ask your mom if you are not sure), stereotyping and prejudice (racism, sexism, homophobia, nationalism – all the -isms), and sensitivity issues (things that are distressing to others, like illness, recent tragedies, etc.).

A significant amount of time in improvisation training and practice is devoted to trying to create direct connections to the imagination, and trying to avoid self-censoring or judging ideas. This creates a unique problem for improvisors as obviously, there are some things one probably shouldn't say.

How do you balance the two? It isn't easy. Remember that *improvisors will perform the way they practice and rehearse*. Being aware of these issues while in training will seep into the performance style. Working toward solving this balancing dilemma while in training is the key to avoiding problems when performing.

It's Your Choice, And Your Consequences

Avoiding certain topics or words altogether, altering a performance style for different audiences, or plowing through as normal, throwing self-censorship to the wind and letting the chips fall where they may, is ultimately the individual improvisor's choice. As a team creative process, the concerns and attitudes of fellow improvisors need to be considered. At the very least, their attitudes and opinions will have an effect on whether they want to work together again.

Children

It is my opinion that altering your performance style (in some cases) to match your audience is not necessarily a bad thing, and does not necessarily indicate that you are selling-out or bowing to pressures such as *political correctness*. In other cases, there are some things I won't do or change on the principle of it.

An obvious case where a particular style and content are needed is one involving *children in the audience*, but even here a grey area starts to quickly emerge. An audience of children usually requires a different performance style, and different content than that for adults. Everybody probably gets that, and most improvisors would dial down to zero the swearing, sexual innuendo, sexuality, and hot button topics like incest, rape, religion, abortion and disturbing violence etc. Performing for young people is a different thing than performing for real humans, and something I have zero interest in doing, personally. So, I avoid these issues by avoiding ever getting up in front of a gaggle of these nasty little cretins.

People Who Bring Kids to Adult Shows

When it gets more difficult is when children have been brought to an adult show. If your improvisation is usually highly uncensored using *mature language and themes*, do you want to change it to avoid exposing the children to inappropriate content? Or, is it the responsibility of the unthinking, inconsiderate adults who brought the children in the first place, to leave if the content is not appropriate? The answer for me is simple: depends.

Please don't bring children to adult improv shows! Even if you are ok with your kids being exposed to mature subject matter, and even if the kids are 'too young to get it' or so hip they are cool with it, the fact remains that having children present at an adult show can be off-putting to both the performers and other audience members, who may feel uncomfortable with children being exposed to mature subject matter.

Parents should always ask in advance if the show is family friendly. If the show is being performed in a bar, or if I am in it, then it is probably not suitable.

Let's Be Grown-Ups

I will focus my discussion then on issues for an audience of grownups. Even within the adult audience world there are different groups; a group of seniors from the local church will likely want a different show than the frat-boys at an on-campus show. (I know I am pushing it a little by including frat-boys in the 'adult' group – but my point stands.) A corporate show for a company at a conference will have different content suitability expectations than would a show for those exact same audience members if they were sitting watching a show in a bar after the conference is finished. As an improvisor, you ignore this fact at your own peril.

Know Your Audience

Know your audience. I am not saying pander to the most sensitive person in the crowd, but if the most sensitive person in the crowd is the CEO of the company at a corporate show, offending this person could make everyone else uncomfortable, and it will have a direct effect on the success or failure of the performance.

Knowing your audience means taking a look at them before the show. Knowing your audience is being aware of any particular groups that have come together (Has a group of friends come together to celebrate someone's birthday? Are there are group of women together for a *Hen Night*, or *Stagette*? Are the *Masons* in town? Has there been a mass escape at the local prison? etc. etc.) Knowing your audience is being aware of the community you are performing in. Knowing your audience means being mindful of the audiences's response to the show, and adapting as you go; if they are not laughing at the dick jokes, maybe they don't like dick jokes. Probably not a bad idea to try something else. That's the beauty of improv: if something is not working, you can improvise!

I remember as a child going to some community event, and there was a stand up comic doing a little routine just before our city mayor was scheduled to speak. The jokes were a little vaudeville and hackneyed, I am sure, but I was a kid so it was all new to me. The comedian was making some somewhat sexist jokes about the mayor hitting on the sexy secretaries at our city hall (remember this was a while ago, when I was a kid, back then this was 'funny'). The audience was not laughing, and even as a kid I could see how uncomfortable the comedian was becoming. His discomfort made me uncomfortable. He started to panic and rush through his material. Even as a kid I could tell what was happening, and I remember it to this day.

He was bombing, and he didn't know why. The audience was not laughing, but *not* because they were offended. It was because they knew this guy had no idea who the mayor was, and could see through his story about 'being down at city hall the other day' as a completely hack bit he had done a thousand times before.

Our mayor was a woman. Know your audience.

Be In Control

With all these hot-button issues, as well as anything else that happens on stage, the important thing is that *the audience must always feel that they are in the hands of experts*, or at the very least competent practitioners of comedy who will not accidently let the show die with an offensive line, an inappropriate reference, or a boring scene. If the audience feels safe and secure in the fact that you know what you are doing, they will allow you all sorts of leeway as far as topics and language, assuming (hopefully correctly) that your choice of topic or language was necessary for the comedy to be brilliant, and that you are aware of any potentially objectionable material, and have an inspired tactic in store of making what might otherwise be distasteful, *surprising pleasant.*

Racism and Stereotypes

Avoid racism and sexism. Next.

Hold up. It isn't as easy as all that. Especially in improv. One person's racism is another person's lovingly self-depreciatingly take on their own 1/16 ethnic heritage.

In short, avoid racial stereotypes, especially when you are starting out in improv. Always play at the top of your intellect, and do not rely on the racial stereotypes to be the funny bit: That is someone else's joke already. Race can be used, and be played for comedic purposes in improvisation, but it requires a great deal of self-awareness.

Racial or Racist

What is the difference between racial and racist? Can an improvisor play a character of a race other than her own without being guilty of racism? I say yes. But....

This is not an easy question, so let me use something slightly different by way of an example for the purpose of exploration. I don't have the answers. I think the answers lie in understanding and exploring the question.

Playing Cross Gender

In improv, improvisors will, out of necessity, sometimes play a character that is a different sex than their own. Sometimes, we really camp it up: picture a guy playing a gal in a date scene with another improvisor who is also a guy. The guy playing the gal might really play up a whole whack of female stereotypes (flipping her hair, putting on her make-up, fussing with her bra, etc.), having fun with the fact that he is obviously a guy playing a woman in a scene that is, at heart, a romance scene and therefore by extension sexual. Sex, sexuality and gender are part of the basis of the scene because the characters are on a date, and this improvisor (for good or bad) had decided to try to milk what he can from the fact that he is not actually a woman, and everyone knows it.

But in an other scene, two improvisors may be doing a scene in a restaurant that calls for a server to come and deliver some drinks. Why would a female improvisor come on stage as a male waiter, or visa versa? Maybe just because the mood struck her, which is fair enough. But because this scene is not about dating, then sex, sexuality and gender are not important, and you may find the female improvisor portrays the male waiter much more naturalistically, lowering her voice a little and walking with a recognizable male gait, but other than that not getting involved in any over-the-top male stereotypes (crassness like scratching his ass, or adjusting his package, or being a sexist brute that leers and makes inappropriate comments, etc.) She is more focused on just being a waiter rather than being a woman who is playing a (male) waiter.

Two different approached to playing cross gender. One (the first) might be accused of being sexist because of the use of broad stereotypes, while the other, being more subtle and not intending to make any commentary on the nature of being male, may not be considered sexist.

Choosing To Portray Anything Is A Choice

But still, because the female improvisor in the second instance has chosen to be a male, it will be noticed. She could have just as easily come into the scene as a waitress, and because the gender of the character doesn't matter necessarily in this scene in the same way it does in a scene about romance, the audience can't help but look for clues to *why* she made this choice. The other improvisors may also take this as indication of some grander motive other than just 'she felt like it' (which again, is a completely legitimate reason.) Likewise, if you choose to play any race or ethnic group other than your own, no matter how subtly and honestly you portray it, the audience will notice it, and be on guard for anything that is derogatory as an indication of your racist intent.

Was she sexist, assuming that a server must be male? Was the male improvisor sexist by indulging over-the-top female stereotypes? And what if, rather than gender we were discussing race?

Recognize Your Own Prejudices

If someone calls for a nurse, and a male improvisor chooses to come on as a female, maybe he needs to admit that that was a sexist choice. However, if the scene is set in the 1930s, then maybe it was the right choice, as that was true to the 1930s. If a character works at some given profession and an improvisor chooses to be a character of a race that is associated with that particular profession (I think of cab-drivers who, depending where you live, are 'always' such-and-such) then maybe it was a racist choice.

It is more probable that the choice was sexist or racist if it was made without even thinking. If the choice is on purpose, to make a point, comedic, political or otherwise, then perhaps the choice is defendable. (See the section on *Irony* later).

The Real Question: Offensive or Not

The real question is, *was it offensive*? For me this is what matters. Remember that this is comedy, and as such you do need to cut a little bit more slack than you would in other situations. It *is* possible for a male to play a woman in a way that is not sexistly offensive, and visa versa. It *is* possible to play another race or ethnic group in a way that is non-offensive. It may be, technically, racist or sexist, but, with some guile, subtly, wit, and self-awareness, there is lots of comedy to be found in gender, racial and ethnic issues and portrayals -- comedy that does not need to demean or disparage any particular identifiable group.

I strongly disagree with anyone who feels that you should *never* play cross gender or a race or ethnic group other than your own, or that you should never make a joke about sex or race. Not everyone will agree with me on this. Damn immigrants!

The Gays

The same sensitivity one needs to utilize with issues of gender and race goes for sexual orientation. If you still think that being gay is comedy, then I suggest you go back to where you came from, like 1970. Unfortunately, at the time of writing this, there are still a lot of people who are really uncomfortable with homosexuality. This *discomfort* is, in my opinion, fair game for comedy, satire, and ridicule and is one of the only places from which *homosexuality* should be safely mined for comedy. Just be careful that you really *are* making fun of, or exposing to the light of day, the societal and/or the audience's uneasiness with homosexuality, and not just making fun of homosexuals.

What You Do, Not Who You Are

That's not to say homosexuals, or any unique group, racial, ethnic, age related, profession related or otherwise, don't do a lot of hilariously stereotypical things that can be used for comedic purposes. But if you are making fun of what a group of people *does*, make *sure* you are making fun of what they *do*, not what they *are*, and that the humour comes from a place of *love* and *respect*. And in some way you need to let the audience know *that you know* that all members of a group are not the same, and any trait you are satirizing is not necessarily indicative of everyone in that group. All lawyers are not liars, for example. (Without limiting the generality of the forgoing, hitherto, and forthwith, further references to the said group ('lawyers', hereafter referred to as 'law professionals') shall, pursuant to my own advice, and without prejudice, cease and desist.)

How do you let the audience *know you know?* First, you gotta know it. Second, not playing into, or relying on, the basest assumptions of hackneyed stereotypes will also indicate that you are coming at the issue from a deeper, more mindful place.

If the humour can not come from love (like when you are satirizing Nazis, bullies, prudes, or arrogant assholes, for example), then be damn sure this group fully deserves any derision you are heaping on them for the behaviours they exhibit based on decisions they have made.

Shock verses Schlock

Be able to do an entire show without swearing even once if you need to. If you can't, work on it until you can.

Then swear where you need to.

If you are very vulgar it needs to be clearly a character trait of the character you are portraying, or very funny, or both.

Swearing can get a laugh through the *surprise* it creates, the *shock value.* To get the most *shock value,* it needs to be truly unexpected and used sparingly. Use some imagination when swearing. Make up some good ones.

Using vulgarity is not the same as relying on vulgarity. Do not *rely* on vulgarity. The audience quickly sees through and tires of improvisors that *rely* on vulgar sexuality to get a laugh. Use it, by all means. Doesn't bother me. (I love it.) But what bothers me, and everybody else, is someone who *tries* to be funny by swearing, or being sexual and *fails*. Remember that. (You shouldn't be trying to be funny anyway... but whatever.)

There is no quicker way to experience the silent awfulness of a soured audience than relying on a vulgar sexual gag that fails. It is so desperate, so pathetic. Yikes! It burns.

And finally, only use vulgarity and sexual references that you are comfortable with. If it makes you uneasy to say, then the audience will sense it, feel uncomfortable, and resent you for making them feel that way.

You Can't Please Everyone, Don't Resent It

Your intellectual understanding of something is trumped by someone else's emotional real-life experiential understanding in every case, at least in their mind. You do jokes about the 9/11 twin tower attacks, having waited 'long enough' so as to give everyone time to process the shock of the event, and having intellectualized the importance of confronting unpleasant situations in comedy as a way of healing and exploring socio-political realities that lead to the blaa blaa blaa, *don't mean nothing* to someone in your audience who lost someone in the attack. Period. It is not funny to them. It doesn't matter what your argument is: *comedy helps society to heal, etc*. If the audience member isn't buying it, he isn't buying it. He has every right not to buy it; he is under no obligation to have 'gotten over it by now'. Your abstract argument about the nature of comedy is irrelevant, because his experience is not abstract. In a case like this, there is nothing to do but accept their ire, apologize if they confront you, back away, and think about it. Whatever you do, don't argue your comedy. Explain what you hoped you were doing, if you must, but don't argue, then shut up. Accept that they do not appreciate your humour. Do not expect everyone to share your sensibilities. People who do not share your sensibilities on hot-button topics are probably more 'normal' than you are, so don't get too high up on your horse because this or that doesn't offend you. *You* are the one that made the 9/11 joke; to be surprised that *some* people find it inappropriate shows a lack of basic understanding of humanity, and I would suggest you look into that.

No One Has a Right Never To Be Offended

But for some things, you need to stand your ground. Comedy can not survive if it tries to please everyone. If you feel religion or politics or abortion rights or 9/11 or whatever are fair topics for comedy regardless of how emotionally charged they are, and you are willing to stand by your conviction on this, then by all mean, do. Just don't be surprised if it pisses some people off. For me, I always ask myself *who* will it piss off, and do they deserve it? And do I care? Grieving widows? Do they deserve to be upset as the cost of my comedy? Probably not. But Nazi's or skinheads or other hate groups? Is it ok that I cast them in a bad light or expose them to ridicule? Indeed. How about politicians that seem to care little about the effect some specific policy will have on others? Do I need to be sensitive about offending them? Not likely.

You will offend people. Some people act like they have a *right* not to be offended. They do not.

Political Correctness

Our modern culture is far more sensitive in many ways than in previous generations, which is a good thing in general. Of course I am annoyed with out-of-control political correctness as much as anyone, and given my particular sense of humour, I often find myself on the far side of someone else's line of what is appropriate. I am okay with that. I think my security in my position comes from the fact that I have a very good idea of where *my* line is. Not only do I know where it is, I am confident that my line strikes the right balance of sensitivity and respect for freedom of expression, with a perfectly correct amount of slack given for comedy's sake. That's how I feel, anyway. My line shifts a bit over time and based on what I experience, but at any given time, I am aware of where I last saw it. I am also willing to forgive myself (even if others can not) when I do inadvertently step over my own line. It happens. I'm human, just like the great masses of those who are inferior to me.

I try to avoid ridiculing victims, and to focus my satirical assaults on poking fun at *behaviours that come from choices* rather than those things which cannot be changed. It's the difference between making fun of the guy who shoots himself while being an idiot and juggling a loaded gun, and the guy who shoots himself committing suicide. I see the first as potential fodder for comedy, and the second one as not. But that's just me. And I don't always succeed in making the right choices. A whole lot of offensive, sexist, racist, homophobic, insensitive, mean-spirited, unthinking, unimaginative crap has popped out of my mouth on stage in the heat of the passion of the excitement of the moment. But I do try not to.

The Insensitivities of the Sensitive

And then, of course, there are those who are *oversensitive*. There are some people that I swear must enjoy being offended in some weird way; people who are not actually offended themselves, but are offended for others. These people are the people that like to write letters, and complain, and try to get people fired. They are hard to deal with. Avoiding and ignoring them is one approach. The other approach is to make sure they know that you heard their complaint. Much of the time that is what they really want; they want you to know how much of a non-racist they are by pointing out how such-and-such a line in one improvised scene 40 minutes ago might be taken the wrong way. Tell them they have a good point, and thank them for bringing it to your attention and that you will think about it and really try to keep what they are saying in mind. Then either do that, or ignore what they said. Up to you.

Irony

There are improvisors who defend their offensive attempts at comedy with the argument that they are being *ironic*. They need to figure out what irony is and what it isn't. (And while they are at it, look up the differences between *sarcastic* and *facetious* and then tell me if they really do 'like sarcastic humour'.) Then there are those who tell me they like insulting humour. Idiots!

Irony needs to be clearly ironic, or it's not irony. Don't try to shield nastiness, hateful or prejudice ideas behind the defense of being *ironic*. Simply saying you were being *ironic* when you chose to make your ethnic character a lazy, stupid, illegal alien, who smells bad and steals, does not justify the fact that your were just being racist, offensive, unimaginative, and relying on old stereotypes.

What is *ironic* is that those who think they are being *ironic* and are actually being prejudice are easily and immediately recognized by the audience for what they truly are, and now the audience knows something about someone on stage that the person on stage does not know about themselves. *Dramatic irony irony irony.*

Use 100% Of Your Brain

In all cases, whether it is hot-button, emotionally charged, racy, sexy, dirty, or run-of-the-mill everyday topics, always play at the top of your game. Always use the best of your intellect. Always be as smart as you can be, even when you are being silly, stupid and juvenile. Don't rely on hackneyed ideas. Show us how smart you are. Audiences love to be in the presence of sharp wit. Dull people get the abhorrence they deserve.

They say we only use 10% of our brains, the other 90% is reserved for use by improvisors in the heat of the stage moment!

Don't Be Desperate

I have devoted so much time to these difficult subject matters of racism, sexism, sexual orientation, vulgarity and the like because for many beginning improvisors this proves to be a very difficult thing to grasp: what you can get away with saying and what you can't. So often beginner improvisors, in a desperate attempt to get a laugh, grasp at vulgarity or taboo topics, and when not rewarded with the laugh they have seen others receive for similar attempts, don't understand why they failed.

There are many reasons why a vulgar or off-colour joke didn't get a laugh. And in trying to solve this we are slipping into *'how to be funny'* rather than how to do improv. There is rarely an occasion when an improvisor steps into one of these mine-fields as part of a scene without deliberately *trying* to be funny. It is this *intentional* attempt at humour that when spotted, and especially when accompanied by vulgarity or an inappropriate topic, that often results in comedic failure.

Don't try to be funny. As Yoda used to joke, "Be funny or don't be funny, there is no trying to be funny."

It takes either a natural ability to get away with some types of racy humour, which, if you are having the difficulties I have just describes, you do not have; or, it takes a lot of experience.

But remember, you will never be funny.

THE AUDIENCE

Them

It has come time to discuss the others that are involved in the experience of doing improv; the ones who sit there in the dark, hoping to be entertained. Them: *The audience* (from the Greek word *audienciapadopolous* which means *to wait for half-price tickets or a pay-what-you-can night.*) The audience plays a vital role in improv comedy.

In any type of live show, the audience actually influences the performance in subtle, and sometimes not-so-subtle ways. The audience, although not on stage (though in improv, sometimes they are) is part of the show. They need to be included in the thought process of the performers.

Feeding Off Of Audience Energy

In a very disciplined and highly rehearsed performance, such as a ballet, each performance may seem identical to the untrained eye. But ask the dancers or the director or choreographer of a show, and they will tell you that a crowd that is demonstrating their enjoyment (through applauding, or being quiet when they should, etc.) will shape the performance of the dancers. The dancers will give a little bit more, a little bit extra. We thespians call it *feeding off of the audience's energy.* A rock band might actually change what songs they perform, or do more songs, or longer versions, if it becomes obvious to them that the crowd is really into it. Improv is also highly influenced by their audience, perhaps more so than most other art forms.

The Audience As Part of the Show

In improv, the influence an audience has on the show is a lot less subtle than, say, with dance. In most forms of improv comedy, the audience is actively utilized in some way as part of the show. Often, at the very least, the audience is mined for *starting suggestions* for a scene. This is done for two main reasons:

Proof

Firstly, *audience suggestions* serve to *prove* that what they are witnessing *is improvised.* It's the equivalent of the magician's, "Have we ever met before?" Ultimately, the goal of improv is to make it all seem effortless, and magical;

we want the audience to doubt that what they saw was made up on the spot; we want the audience to find it *so* impossible that they saw what they saw, that they don't believe they saw what they did. We improvisors want the audience en masse to evaporate in a sudden blast of euphoric disbelief at the inventiveness of our on-stage shenanigans. We want brains to melt and heads to pop open. We want urine-filled trousers! We want all sorts of weird stuff.

And to achieve it, we must give the audience something that really messes with their minds. By taking *audience suggestions and using them* we are proving that what they are seeing has been improvised, and messing with them by doing something so wonderful with their suggestion that there is no way it was *not* pre-planned and rehearsed. That's the goal anyway.

Make Them Part of The Show

The second reason to utilize the audience, is to make them a part of the show. This is done because we need them to play along for the show to work. We need to use their imaginations to create the stage picture for them. Without sets, and costumes, and lighting, and special effects and all the things that, say, a movie has at its disposal to create a story for its audience, improvisors rely on the audience's imaginations to fill in the spaces between the improvisors on stage. The audience is a necessary part of improv comedy, and as such they need to feel ownership in what is being created for them. We give them that sense of ownership by using suggestions, or even using audience members as part of the show.

Use Their Suggestions!

And the audience is willing to play along (some audiences more actively than others) but do so at a cost. In return for buying into the show, the audience expects two things. The first, and the simplest, is that if they are asked for a *suggestion* they want it used! Nothing makes an audience feel cheated faster than when an *audience suggestion* is not used in a scene. The more integral the *audience suggestion* is to the plot, environment, and/or main characters of the scene, the more rewarding it is for the audience. A great scene that fails to use an *audience suggestion* or used the *audience suggestion* in only a cursory way, may be less enthusiastically received than a less stellar scene that really exploited the *audience suggestion* and made it vital to the plot of the scene.

Protect the Civilians

The second thing that an audience demands for playing along is: they want to come out of the experience better off than they were before. It is this demand that is the source of resistance from audience members who do not want to shout out suggestions, or do not want to join the improvisors on stage for a scene; they are concerned that they will make a fool of themselves, or worse, that the improvisors will make a fool of them. You will see it, with audiences taking seats at the back of the room because they don't want to be 'picked on' by sitting up front. This is something they may have learned from going to other forms of comedy, like standup, that often relies on a combative form of audience interaction for material, with heckling and counter-heckling, insults and the like.

I don't think that is valuable for improv.

Remember that the audience members are *civilians* and we are the *improv warriors*. We have the training, the equipment, and the armour to tackle the main danger of improv, namely, *the danger of making an ass of yourself.*

I strongly believe that you must never put an audience member in a situation where they look like an ass. That doesn't mean you can't have fun, or make fun of them, but again, the same sensitivity that applies when dealing with issues of race, gender, and what have you, need to apply here as well. You can lovingly make fun of what an audience member *does* or *says*, as long as you are not making fun of what they are.

Never

You need to care for the civilian. Never leave a civilian on stage alone. Never leave the success of the scene up to the civilian having to come up with something clever; the scene should be able to be successful regardless of the input the audience member is capable of adding. Your job is to make the audience member *look* clever, regardless of what a complete imbecile he really is. Never *really* criticize an audience member's performance or suggestion; you can have fun, 'taking the piss' as the Brits might say, with a bit of counterfeit criticism, of course. But make sure you realize that even doing *this* may have the undesired consequence of having other audience members less eager to offer up a suggestion or get involved.

Minimize Real Risk

Any involvement by an audience member in the show involves a risk of looking like an ass for the audience member; after all, they don't know what you are planning to do. Perhaps they have never seen improv before. You must minimize the risk to zero. Remember there will always be a *perceived* risk by the audience member, so having no *real* risk will not diminish the thrill for the audience or the audience member on stage with you. (No one rides a rollercoaster because there is a risk that it was constructed by incompetent idiots, and that it might fall apart. We ride it because, while we know it is 100% safe, it still seems scary as hell.) Just as I would not get on a rollercoaster that is not safe, I wouldn't want to join improvisors on stage if doing so posed any risk of having to endure real ridicule.

I personally don't like fire-jugglers, or magicians or street performers that put audience members in real physical danger, you know, getting them to lie down while the performer juggles knives above them. I get that it makes it exciting, but I can't get past the fact that if something goes wrong, it is the audience member that gets a knife in the face. I hate it, and I would never volunteer to be one of these performer's victims. Improv that uses an audience member, in my opinion, is not so much about the thrill that comes from seeing the audience member in danger, as it might be in a fire-sword-chainsaw juggling act, but rather, in the thrill that comes from seeing what improvisors are able to do with the unexpected element that *is* the audience member, and how good the improvisors can make the audience member look on stage. It is fine that the *improvisors* are in danger by having a loose-cannon audience member on stage, because after all, they are trained improv warriors.

Make the Audience Member the Hero

And, ultimately, the audience member must become a *improv war hero* as a result of getting involved. Even if it means just thanking an audience member for shouting out a suggestion from the darkened room, make their involvement rewarding!

If other audience members aren't coming up after the show to an audience member who joined you on stage to congratulate her on how amazing she was, then you have failed miserably in caring for the civilian.

You need your audience. You need to nurture your audience. You need to love your audience.

What The Audience Sees

Because of their position, physically in front of all the action, and because of their position figuratively as outside of the action, the audience's perception is very different from that of the performers on stage. I often tell beginner improvisors that *the audience can see everything*. They see when things are forgotten, when opportunities are missed, they see the mistakes. They notice when an audience suggestion is not used. They can see through improvisors who are being lazy, or unspecific, or who are trying to hide insecurities or overcompensate for something. They see it all. I tell beginner improvisors all this, not to scare them, but to motivate them to resist sloppiness. It does scare some though. Ah well.

What the audience can't see is how the stuff that works is done!

The audience remembers where mimed doors and objects are. Because you have asked them to do that creative imagination work for you in their heads, you will find them disappointed and feeling cheated if you later, carelessly walk through where a mimed table was previously established or absent-mindedly change a character's name.

An audience can be very perceptive, and I recommend that you treat your audience with an expectation of this perceptiveness.. until a given audience proves otherwise. To do the opposite, to behave as if you expect the audience to be a mob of unthinking goobers, is probably not going to serve you well. Expecting that all audiences will react similarly to the same type of material, for instance, does not show the audience the respect they need to sense from you if you hope to get the best out of them. Audiences are as individual as the individual audience members; each one is unique.

Using the Audience, Choose Your Words

Because of this perceptiveness in the audience, you might find yourself accidently cuing them for the wrong thing. For example, if you want a suggestion from the audience, make sure you word your request carefully. If you ask, “What is something two roommates might fight about?” the audience may expect the next scene to be about two roommates fighting. If you were just using that question as a way to inspire them to think of something, you may want to make it clear that the scene will not necessarily be about fighting roommates. If you ask for an everyday object, like a *knife* or a *fork*, they may suggest *spoon, whisk, spatula, tongs*, or other *cutlery*. It might be better to have given a couple of suggestions that are not easy to connect in a category, allowing for more latitude in the audience’s collective mind as to where their idea is apt to originate. *What is an everyday object, like a spoon or a lawnmower?* may still get you a household items, whereas *What is an everyday object, like a spoon, lawnmower, or an office chair?* might signal to the audience (even subconsciously) that they are not limited to items around the *house* only.

Audience Members on Stage

Getting an audience member to join the improvisors on stage to take part in a *game, handle*, or *scene* is one of the mainstays of improv comedy. There are some do's and don'ts for making this go as smoothly as possible, recognizing that this is one of those things that no one every has complete control over, and one can only do one's best.

Start by asking for a volunteer and see what happens. More often than not you end up with people pointing at their friends.

Never Tell The Audience What They Are Needed For

Never tell the audience what you need a volunteer for. You can reassure them of all sorts of things that won't happen, like: we won't make fun of you, you don't have to say anything, or you don't have to do anything, etc. based on what you have in mind for them. Be honest, but don't tell them what they are needed for.

You will find that if they know, they are less likely to get involved. For example, *Can we get a volunteer up here? You will just have to finish ends of our sentences for us.*

"What?! How will I be able to do that? I have to come up with the punchline?" The audience thinks collectively. No one wants to get involved.

Can we get a volunteer? You will be moving us around like puppets.

"Sounds stupid. No thanks," says the audience with their silence.

Even experienced audience members, who have seen improv before and *want* to volunteer may not do so if they know what you need them for, as they try to *hold out* for the one thing they saw before that they would like to try to do.

Always just ask for a volunteer, reassuring them honestly of how well it will go, and alleviating fears if need be.

The Skill of Picking the Right "Volunteer"

Often you will ask for someone to volunteer, but no one does. That is when you have to *pick a 'volunteer'*, and cajole someone onto the stage.

By *often*, I mean *<u>often</u>*.

There is a bit of a skill in finding the right *volunteer*. You want someone who is not so totally terrified that being on a stage would be a traumatic and awful experience; and also not the 'funny guy' from work who is a little too eager to be 'talked into it' and wants to show everyone in the audience who he came with how comedy is really done by regaling us all with his long list of racist, sex-jokes about the handicapped.

Check out the crowd as they come in, and from the sidelines or backstage during the show. Someone who is not laughing ever, not a good choice probably. Someone who is laughing too much... also bad. Find the friendly face, and try to never use other improvisors! Trust me.

Sometimes people will actually *volunteer*, and there will only be one person. You go with what you got.

The Surprise of the Expected

The audience loves to be surprised (pleasantly), but they also love to see what they hope will happen, happen.

I am talking about situations where there is an expectation of something being said or done, and then when it transpires, it makes the audience laugh. Using the audience suggestion falls into this category. Take this as an example. The audience suggestion is a *smelly old sock*. The scene begins and a husband, excited about something, informs his wife he has a surprise for her. "What is it?" she asks. He really plays it up, making her close her eyes and put out her hands, and with a grandiose "Happy Anniversary" hands her – "It's a smelly old sock." The audience, who know full well that the audience suggestion (given 15 second earlier) was *a smelly old sock*, still burst into laughter. Perhaps they were surprised that *this* is how the suggestion was utilized. But there is more to it than that, because before it was revealed that the anniversary gift was the sock, the audience started to titter in anticipation. While some audience members may have been completely surprised, many, if not most, knew exactly what was about to happen. You can feel it on stage, when the audience has caught on to what is happening, and are able to predict the outcome.

When the audience gets to witness what they hoped would happen, they experience something cathartic, which is, of course, pleasant. I also think the audience is surprised by how cathartic it can be. It can be a very weird thing to experience as an improvisor on stage, feeling an audience's anticipation build, knowing that by giving them exactly what they know you are going to give them, they are going to burst into laughter; like knowing this chapter will inevitably end with a demoralizing comment about your lack of potential to one day achieve funniness.

And you will never be funny.

SOME FINAL THOUGHTS

This is Art, Not Science

Improv is an art not a science. There is no exact way to do improv, it is personal and individual and as unique as you keep telling yourself you are. I think I may have mentioned that you will never be funny, and that no one can teach you to be funny. Funny is one of those artistic sparks that you have or you don't. You've been around truly funny people before, you know what I am talking about.

The *craftsmanship* of improv can be taught to some degree however, and it is that which I have attempted to begin to do here in this book.

Great craftsmanship involves study, and practice, and the good news is that we all have some degree of control over how much we study and how much we practice. If you want to be a great craftsperson, study and practice a great deal.

Remember to remember things. It is so easy, in the heat of the moment on stage, for all that you have studied to fly out the window and you revert to some panicked response. If that happens, then the practice you end up doing is practicing stuff the wrong way. Be *mindful*, especially as you begin doing improv. Think about what you have been taught and try to apply it; then go over what you did in your mind to see what worked and what didn't. But, never beat yourself up over 'mistakes' you made. The moment is past. The scene or exercise is over. Just don't do what you did 'wrong' ever again.

Cut yourself some slack. Improv can be very, very hard. Tighten the slack over time.

Let me know if this helps:

> *Not doing what you have been taught to do, will not help you to discover anything; doing what you have been taught not to do, will help you to discover nothing about what to do; and, doing nothing, will not help you discover what doing what you were taught, will do.*

There Are No Rules In Improv

There are no rules to improv, and here they are:

> Stay in the moment.
>
> Don't pre-plan.
>
> Listen actively.
>
> Be willing to give up control: Pass control back and forth.
>
> Never say *no*.
>
> Define *who, where* and *what* as *specifically* and as quickly as possible.
>
> When you don't know what to say, say *yes*. See what happens.

Remember that stuff?

Exceptions

There is an exception to everything. There are no *rules* to improv; there are just guidelines, and helpful and not-so-helpful advice. Do not take anything I say in this book as a *rule*. Not only are there lots of exceptions, not everyone who is experienced in improv will agree with me on many things. I am pretty confident with my opinions on stuff, however, and will challenge anyone to prove me fundamentally wrong. But there are definitely different schools of thought, and I belong to one, and have been suspended or expelled from others.

But don't go out looking for the exceptions. They will find you soon enough. Shoot for developing the right habits first.

Take Your Time

Much of what you can learn about improv can only be learned by actually doing improv. Unfortunately, in some ways, improv requires an audience. It is not something that can be done in a vacuum. You might be able to learn how to be a fantastic ballet dancer without ever stepping a weird misshapen foot in front of an audience, but that is simply not possible with improv comedy. You need to get in front of people for it to be what it is.

For the time being, those that you are studying with, and training with, must serve as the audience. It will have to do for now.

The risk is that, by rushing, you will get in front of an audience before you are ready. It's risky for you, the audience and improv in general. And, admittedly there are many times that improvisors do step out in front of a crowd before they should, and it does nobody any good. Even the reputation of improv suffers from it. But a time will come when you need to feel the energy of the crowd to understand why you should even bother with this. For improv to be improv, it needs that audience there. Don't fear it, love it! You will have a lot of fun.

So, be patient. Practice. Take workshops. Do not rush to the stage. It will be there when you are ready.

This is Just The Beginning

There is a lot more to improv than I can force out of my brain into my laptop. This book only scratches the surface, but I hope it is a deep and infecting scratch.

Improv has given me endless good times. I love doing it. It is so much fun! It is way better than working in retail. Like 15% better!!!

It is worth sticking with it to one day get up in front of a group of people that laugh at what you do and say... and in a good way!

You Will Never Be Funny

I know there is a lot to remember, and a lot to think about. But a bit of practice and deliberately attempting to try some of the techniques I have described in this book will help you toward your goal. Before a workshop, or before a show, go over in your head a few of the things that you might have learned here. Replant the seeds in your memory just before you start improvising, and maybe a couple might sprout a little and start to grow into the good habits that you need to do improv effortlessly.

If you take only one thing away from this book, let it be this: ***You will never be funny****.

(* If you don't get this joke, then it definitely applies to you.)

APPENDIX

At the beginning of this book I suggested that the principles of improv could be used for purposes outside of the theatre (or the bar). I have not specifically referenced this in the book. Hopefully those who are looking for insight into how improv can be used in the business world are able to extrapolate what I have said in reference to performance and are able to imagine adaptations for their own workplace.

To this end, I have included a little taster of what improv can bring to the business world. What follows is a short article which I wrote for www.taskworld.com, an online project management suite of tools. This article addresses directly the possibility of using improv principles in the workplace. The article is reprinted here with permission.

YES! The Golden Rule of Comedy Is Relevant to Business

By Drew McCreadie, www.taskworld.com

Learning A Lesson From Comedy

Improvisational comedy is comedy made up on the spot, with a group of actors walking on stage with little or no idea what they are about to say. For many people, (even including many professional actors), this idea is terrifying. Public speaking is widely recognized as the number one greatest fear, so the idea of speaking in public without pre-preparation verges on insanity. Glorious insanity for those who do it well. What is the secret, and is there anything that the business world can learn? The answer is *yes*!

Perfectly Synced Teamwork

Improv comedy is not complete recklessness, in fact, when done to the highest levels it is an example of excellent teamwork. Imagine three or four people working together to tell a story that no one has heard before. Improv achieves this by conforming to a set of rules; rules that can be adopted and used by project managers to achieve what improv comedy troupes are able to achieve, namely, *unbounded creativity* and *perfectly syncing teamwork*. The first, and foremost of these is *Saying Yes.*

Yes! The Antidote To Stagnation And Ego

On stage, improv actors will say *yes* to any idea offered by a fellow actor. This leads to the story *moving forward*, and helps to eliminate any *ego conflicts* that might arise from the suggestion that, by saying *no*, the idea is not a good one, or that someone else has a better idea. Likewise, by saying *yes* in the business world, these same two benefits can also be realized, that is:

forwarding the project through creativity and avoiding ego conflicts.

Resist The Urge To Say NO.

Of course saying *yes* does not mean agreeing to any stupid idea that pops out of some team-members mouth. Rather, it is actively resisting our natural instinct to say *no* as a first response. Consider this situation by way of example:

> A team-member approaches the project manager with a new idea.
>
> "Hey boss, I was thinking we could get our weekly reports out faster if we switched the deadline to Thursdays instead of Fridays, which would allow the overseas members another day to work on them."
>
> "No, that might lead to some scheduling difficulties," replies the manager.
>
> "Oh, ok," responds the team-member.
>
> "But let me think about it," is the manager's final response.

Although the manager has a reasonable concern, in this example that any changes might effect scheduling, his approach is very negative, and has the unwanted side effect of stifling innovative thinking on the part of his team-members. Even though the manager has agreed to think about it, and is perhaps interested in the potential benefits, the instinctual response of saying *no* throws a wet blanket on the team-member's ideas, extinguishing any creative spark that might be kindling. Compare to this approach:

> The team-member makes the same suggestion, but this time the manager replies:
>
> "Oh yeah? Good idea. How would we avoid scheduling difficulties?"
>
> "We could work around those by having the media team here work on Saturday and take Monday off," suggests the team-member.
>
> "Great, let me think about it," is the manager's final response.

By simply saying *yes*, the manager in this example has rewarded the team-member for innovative thinking by giving a positive response. The objection of scheduling difficulties is then turned into a challenge that must be overcome by the team-member; throwing the ball back into the team-member's court, but in a positive way. If, after thinking about it, the manager still decides not to take the suggestion, at least the team-member feels his suggestion was valued and was considered by the manager.

Say Yes First, No Can Come Later

By simply saying *yes* first, and letting the reasons for not adopting a suggestions expose themselves (if they exist) rather than stopping innovation in the bud with a negative response, creativity is allowed to flourish, innovative thinking is rewarded, and ego conflicts are avoided by making every member of the team feel valued.

ABOUT THE AUTHOR

Have you ever wondered who writes the *About The Author* section of a book?

I will give you a hint: He is incredibly handsome, sexy and brilliant; he has written several books and plays including *The Cat Who Ate Her Husband*, which won a bucketful of awards, so that should impress you, and the holiday farce, *The Hotel Bethlehem*. He has written for television, cartoons, comic books, radio (as if anyone cares about that) and film, including his also-award-winning film *The Valet*, which won him a best director award, and several best foreign film awards at a couple of international film festivals that you will have actually heard of if you are into international film festivals. He has performed improv around the world as a member of *Theatresports, Urban Improv, Rock Paper Scissors* (with whom he performed for Canadian and International troops in Kabul, Afghanistan), *The Comedy Club Bangkok*, and for over a year lived *the life* on cruise-ships in the Caribbean performing with *The Second City*. He currently lives in Bangkok, Thailand.

Any ideas?

Also by ***Drew McCreadie***

The Cat Who Ate Her Husband The Play

The award winning play now available in paperback.

Hotel Bethlehem A Holiday Farce

A Holiday Farce. The hit farce now available.

Go Get Help A Self Help Book

Makes a great gift for people who need a self help book. It tells you that if you need help, go get it.

A Test Case of Life A Novel

A political romance wherein life is revealed as a series of uncontrollable coincidences, then the book ends.

All available at ***amazon.com***

Made in the USA
Coppell, TX
08 July 2025

Canadian Comedy Award winning improvisor
Drew McCreadie

Improv comedy is comedy made up on the spot, with a team of improvisors inventing a scene right before the audience's eyes.

For many people, even professional actors, this idea is terrifying, verging on insanity. Glorious insanity for those who do it well!

Learn to do it.

With over twenty years experience as a professional improvisor, Drew McCreadie will take you through the first steps towards a life that is way better than the one you have now!